WJEC Eduqas GCSE (9–1)

English Language

Revision Workbook

Series Consultant: Harry Smith

Authors: Julie Hughes and David Grant

Reviewer: Esther Menon

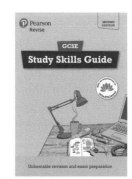

Contents

1-to-1 page match with the Revision Guide
ISBN 9781447988106

Planning your exam time

It is important to use your time wisely in the exam. Look closely at the examples of exam-style questions below. **You don't need to answer these questions.** Instead, look at the marks and think about how long you should spend answering each type of question.

Component

ime allowed: 45 minutes

Read lines 8–14.

A2. How does the writer show what Shukhov's daily routine is like? **(5 marks)**

You must refer to the language used in the text to support your answer.

Read lines 20–33.

A3. What impressions do you get of life in the labour camp from these lines? **(10 marks)**

You must refer to the text to support your answer.

Component

ime allowed: 2 hours

Read the magazine article ''Appy ever after' by John Arlidge.

A1. (a) How hot was it in Goldwasser's office? **(1 mark)**
(b) How many electrodes does Arlidge have attached to his head? **(1 mark)**
(c) How small will the consumer version of the electrodes be? **(1 mark)**

To answer the following questions you will need to use both texts.

A5. According to these two writers, in what ways can a person's mind or mood be altered? **(4 marks)**

A6. Both of these texts are about the ability to control the mind. Compare the following:
- the writers' attitudes to the way the mind can be altered
- how they get across their arguments. **(10 marks)**

1 How many minutes should you spend reading the source texts and questions before you start each exam? . . . .

2 How many minutes should you spend on Component 1, Question A2? . . . .

3 What part of the extract should you refer to in your answer to Component 1, Question A3?

. . . .

4 How many minutes should you spend on each part of Component 2, Question A1?

. . . .

5 How many texts should you use to answer Component 2, Questions A5 and A6?

. . . .

6 Which of the following should you do before you start to answer any of the questions? Circle your choices.

- Read all the questions.
- Skim read the source texts.
- Highlight relevant information in the texts.
- Read the texts a second time.
- Work out how much time you should spend on each question.

Had a go ☐ Nearly there ☐ Nailed it! ☐

Reading texts explained

Read this short extract from *To Kill a Mockingbird*, then answer Question 1 below. Part (a) has been done for you.

> She was horrible. Her face was the colour of a dirty pillowcase, and the corners of her mouth glistened with wet, which inched like a glacier down the deep grooves enclosing her chin. Old-age liver spots dotted her cheeks, and her pale eyes had black pinpoint pupils. Her hands were knobby, and the cuticles were grown up over her fingernails.

Guided

1 (a) Highlight or underline any words or phrases you think create atmosphere.

(b) What type of atmosphere do you think is created here?

....

....

....

....

....

....

....

....

> Read as much and as widely as you can outside lesson time. This will help you start to think about how writers create atmosphere and character.

Now read this short extract from 'Occupations Accessible to Women', then answer Question 2 below.

> Some hard study would, in some cases, be needed to supply the inaccuracy of the general style of a woman's knowledge as a very thorough grounding in elementary subjects is needful. Very few, even the most highly-educated of women, can work a sum in fractions or proportion with rapidity, much less explain every step of the process so clearly as to bring it within the comprehension of a class; and how few who write good English from habit can teach the rules of grammar correctly.

2 (a) Highlight or underline any words or phrases that show the writer's point of view about women's education.

(b) Use your evidence from Question **2** (a) to comment on the author's point of view.

....

....

....

....

....

....

....

....

Reading questions explained 1

There are four assessment objectives in Section A Reading: Assessment objective 1 (AO1), Assessment objective 2 (AO2), Assessment objective 3 (AO3) and Assessment objective 4 (AO4). Read AO1 and AO2 below.

Assessment objective 1
(a) Identify and interpret explicit and implicit information and ideas
(b) Select and synthesise evidence from different texts

Assessment objective 2
Explain, comment on and analyse how writers use language and structure to achieve effects and influence readers, using relevant subject terminology to support their views

Look at the following exam-style questions. **You don't need to answer these questions.** Instead, identify the assessment objective (or the part of the assessment objective) that is being tested and circle it.

Component 1

Read lines 1–10.

A1. List **five** reasons why the children dislike visiting Mrs Dubose. **(5 marks)**

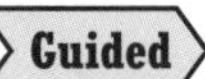
Guided

1 The question above tests:  AO1(a) AO1(b) AO2

Component 2

Read the magazine article ''Appy ever after' by John Arlidge.

A1. (a) How hot was it in Goldwasser's office? **(1 mark)**
(b) How many electrodes does Arlidge have attached to his head? **(1 mark)**
(c) How small will the consumer version of the electrodes be? **(1 mark)**

2 The question above tests: AO1(a) AO1(b) AO2

Component 1

Read lines 22–32.

A4. How does the writer suggest that the children are frightened of Mrs Dubose in these lines? **(10 marks)**
You should write about:
- what happens to suggest they are frightened of Mrs Dubose
- the writer's use of language to suggest their fear
- the effects on the reader.

3 The question above tests: AO1(a) AO1(b) AO2

Component 2

To answer the following question you will need to read the extract 'Victorian Hypnotism' by William James.

A3. (a) What does the writer mean by 'the subject may be shamming' in line 13? **(1 mark)**
(b) What does the writer suggest a hallucination is generally followed by? **(2 marks)**

4 The question above tests: AO1(a) AO1(b) AO2

Component 2

To answer the following question you will need to use both texts.

A5. According to these two writers, in what ways can a person's mind or mood be altered? **(4 marks)**

5 The question above tests: AO1(a) AO1(b) AO2

Had a go ☐ Nearly there ☐ Nailed it! ☐

Reading questions explained 2

Read AO3 and AO4 below.

Assessment objective 3

Compare writers' ideas and perspectives, as well as how these are conveyed, across two or more texts

Assessment objective 4

Evaluate texts critically and support this with appropriate textual references

1 Look at the following exam-style questions. **You don't need to answer them.** Instead, identify the assessment objective that is being tested and circle it.

Component 1

Read lines 22–39.

A5. "In lines 22–39 of this extract, the writer encourages the reader to dislike Mrs Dubose." To what extent do you agree with this view? **(10 marks)**

You should write about:

- your own impressions of Mrs Dubose as she is presented here and in the extract as a whole
- how the writer has created these impressions.

You must refer to the text to support your answer.

(a) The question above tests: AO3 AO4

Component

To answer the following question you will need to read the extract 'Victorian Hypnotism' by William James.

A4. What do you think and feel about William James's view of hypnosis? **(10 marks)**

You should comment on:

- what is said
- how it is said.

You must refer to the text to support your comments.

(b) The question above tests: AO3 AO4

Component

To answer the following question you will need to use both texts.

A6. Both of these texts are about the ability to control the mind. Compare the following:

- the writers' attitudes to the way the mind can be altered
- how they get across their arguments. **(10 marks)**

You must use the text to support your comments and make it clear which text you are referring to.

(c) The question above tests: AO3 AO4

2 Look at the exam-style questions above. Put a tick next to the questions that tell you which lines you should focus on in your answer.

3 If no line numbers are given in the question, how much of the extract text should you use for your answer?

....

Reading the questions

Read the exam-style question below. **You don't need to answer this question.** Instead, think about what it is asking you to do, then answer the questions that follow.

Component 1

Read lines 1–7.

A1. List **five** reasons why the labour camp is an unpleasant place. **(5 marks)**

Guided

1 (a) Highlight or underline:
- the part of the extract you are being asked to use for your answer
- how many pieces of information you are being asked to find
- the focus of the question.

(b) Which word in Question A1 shows that you only need to **find** the reasons, rather than give a full explanation for each one? ....

It is very important to read the questions carefully so that you know which part of the extract to use in your answer.

2 Look at the exam-style questions below. **You don't need to answer these questions.** Instead, annotate each question to show the following information:
- how many texts you need to write about
- how much of each text you should use for your answer
- the key words in the question
- how long you should spend on your answer.

Component 1

Read lines 8–14.

A2. How does the writer show what life is like for Shukhov? **(5 marks)**

You must refer to language used in the text to support your answer.

Component 1

Read lines 20–33.

A4. How does the writer create a sense of despair and hardship in these lines? **(10 marks)**

You should write about:
- what happens to suggest despair and hardship
- the writer's use of language to suggest despair and hardship
- the effects on the reader.

Component 2

To answer the following question you will need to use both texts.

A6. Both of these texts are about teaching. Compare the following:
- the writers' attitudes to teaching and teachers
- how they get across their views. **(10 marks)**

You must use the text to support your comments and make it clear which text you are referring to.

Had a go ☐ Nearly there ☐ Nailed it! ☐

Skimming for the main idea or theme

Read the following extract from 'OK, you try teaching 13-year-olds', then answer the questions below.

OK, you try teaching 13-year-olds

Shocking news: a young trainee languages teacher on placement at Tarleton High in Lancashire "lost it" in class, barricaded the door with furniture, trapping the pupils, and threatened to kill them with something nasty that she had in her handbag.

Guided

1 (a) What does the headline suggest about the main idea or theme of the article?

The headline suggests that the main idea of the article will be the difficulties faced by teachers.

(b) What does the opening sentence suggest about the main idea or theme of the article?

The opening sentence suggests that the main idea will be the difficulties of teaching, although it also suggests ....

....

....

Now read these sentences from the end of the same article, then answer the questions below.

Her career is now ruined. But the children were "petrified … burst into tears" and were offered "support". The pathetic little wets. She was pretending, you fools – dredging up a last desperate ploy to shut the monsters up. If she had cried, they would have laughed out loud. Hopefully, she won't be sacked. If that's what she really, really wants.

2 What does the end suggest about the article's main idea or theme?

....

....

3 Do the ideas expressed at the end of the article differ from those you found at the beginning?

....

....

Skim reading a text can give you a good idea of what it is about before you read it more closely. Look at:

- the headline, title or headings
- the first sentence of each paragraph
- the last sentence of the text.

Turn to the full article, 'OK, you try teaching 13-year-olds', on page 103.
Skim read it for 30 seconds, then answer Question 4.

4 In one sentence, sum up the main idea in the article as a whole.

....

....

....

Annotating the texts

Read this extract from *The Day of the Triffids*. It has been annotated by a student.

> It would have been almost spherical but for three bluntly-tapered projections extending from the lower part. Supported on these, the main body was lifted about a foot clear of the ground.
>
> When it 'walked' it moved rather like a man on crutches. Two of the blunt 'legs' slid forward, then the whole thing lurched as the rear one drew almost level with them, then the two in front slid forward again. At each 'step' the long stem whipped violently back and forth; it gave one a kind of seasick feeling to watch it. As a method of progress it looked both strenuous and clumsy – faintly reminiscent of young elephants at play.

A Simile – sense of the familiar

B Verb and adverb choice reinforces sense of physical danger

C Makes it sound endearing

D Out of control and clumsy movement, potentially dangerous

E Not very big

Now read this exam-style question. **You don't need to answer it.** Instead, think about what it is asking you to do, then answer the questions that follow.

Component ①

Read lines 34–37.

A4. How does the writer make the triffids seem both strange and threatening in these lines? **(10 marks)**

You should write about:

- how the triffids are described to make them seem strange and threatening
- the writer's use of language to suggest they are strange and threatening
- the effects on the reader.

Guided

1 Which of the annotations A to E above would help you to answer Question A4? Circle your choices.

2 Why won't annotation E help you to answer Question A4?

. . . .

. . . .

Now read the rest of the extract from *The Day of the Triffids* on page 98, then answer Question 3.

3 Annotate the extract from *The Day of the Triffids* on page 98, identifying any words or phrases that would help you to answer the exam-style question below. **You don't need to answer the exam-style question itself.**

Component ①

Read line 34 to the end.

A5. "In the last twenty lines or so of this extract, the writer increases the tension as it finally becomes clear that the triffids are dangerous." **(10 marks)**

To what extent do you agree with this view?

You should write about:

- your own impressions of the tension and the way it is increased
- how the writer has created these impressions.

You must refer to the text to support your answer.

Had a go ☐ Nearly there ☐ Nailed it! ☐

Putting it into practice

Read the full extract from *Enduring Love* on page 99, then answer Questions 1 and 2.

1 (a) Highlight, circle or underline any words or phrases in the extract from *Enduring Love* that would help you to answer the exam-style question below.

Component 1

Read lines 15–22.

A3. What impressions do you get of the rescue from these lines? **(10 marks)**

You must refer to the text to support your answer.

(b) Make notes about the effect that each word or phrase you have identified has on the reader.

. . . .

. . . .

. . . .

. . . .

. . . .

. . . .

2 Now use your annotations and notes from Question 1 to write the first two paragraphs of an answer to the exam-style Question A3.

When you tackle this kind of question in the exam, remember to:

- spend about 12 minutes on your answer
- highlight key words in the question so that you get the focus right
- use only the lines of the text referred to in the question.

. . . .

. . . .

. . . .

. . . .

. . . .

. . . .

. . . .

. . . .

. . . .

. . . .

. . . .

. . . .

. . . .

. . . .

. . . .

. . . .

. . . .

Remember: You are only being asked to write part of an answer on this page. In the exam, you will be given more space to write a full answer.

Putting it into practice

Read the full extract from *The Boys Are Back in Town* on page 100, then answer Questions 1 and 2.

1 (a) Highlight, circle or underline any words or phrases in the extract that would help you to answer the exam-style question below.

Component 

A4. What do you think and feel about Simon Carr's views on bringing up children? **(10 marks)**

You should comment on:

- what is said
- how it is said.

You must refer to the text to support your comments.

(b) Make notes about the effect that each word or phrase you have identified has on the reader.

....

....

....

....

....

....

2 Now use your annotations and notes from Question 1 to write the first two paragraphs of an answer to the exam-style Question A4.

When you tackle this kind of question in the exam, remember to:

- spend about 12 minutes on your answer
- highlight key words in the question so that you get the focus right
- focus on the way the ideas and point of view are expressed by the writer.

....

....

....

....

....

....

....

....

....

....

....

....

....

Remember: You are only being asked to write part of an answer on this page. In the exam, you will be given more space to write a full answer.

Had a go ☐ Nearly there ☐ Nailed it! ☐

Explicit information and ideas

Skim read the full article ''Appy ever after' on page 101, then look at the exam-style question below. **You don't need to answer this question.** Instead, think about what it is asking you to do, then answer the questions that follow.

Read the magazine article ''Appy ever after' by John Arlidge.

A1. (a) How many hours' sleep did Arlidge have before arriving at Goldwasser's office? **(1 mark)**
(b) In which town is Goldwasser's office located? **(1 mark)**
(c) What was the temperature when Arlidge arrived at Goldwasser's office? **(1 mark)**

Guided

1 Circle the most effective style of answer for each part (a, b or c) of the exam-style question above.

(a) 7 hours | He had seven hours' sleep.

(b) Goldwasser's office is located in Los Gatos. | Los Gatos

I'm sitting in a picture-book-pretty converted 19th-century opera house that now serves as Goldwasser's office at the centre of Los Gatos, one of the most prosperous towns in Silicon Valley.

(c) It's 10 am but it's already 27°C. | The temperature was 27°C. | 27°C

2 Explain why writing 'I've had seven hours' sleep, coffee and eggs for breakfast' is not the best way to answer Question A1 (a).

....

....

3 Now read the full article 'OK, you try teaching 13-year-olds' on page 103. Then answer the exam-style question below.

A1. (a) At which school was the young teacher working on placement? **(1 mark)**
(b) What age is described by Hanson as 'a particularly cruel age'? **(1 mark)**
(c) How many stitches did Hanson have to have as a result of her car accident? **(1 mark)**

(a) ....

(b) ....

(c) ....

For this type of question, keep your answers as short as possible. Don't copy whole sentences from the extract.

Implicit ideas

Read this short extract from *One Day in the Life of Ivan Denisovich*:

As usual, at five o'clock that morning reveille was sounded by the blows of a hammer on a length of rail hanging up near the staff quarters. The intermittent sounds barely penetrated the window-panes on which the frost lay two fingers thick and then ended almost as soon as they'd begun. It was cold outside, and the camp-guard was reluctant to go on beating out the reveille for long.

The clanging ceased, but everything outside still looked like the middle of the night when Ivan Denisovich Shukhov got up to go to the bucket. It was pitch dark except for the yellow light cast on the window by three lamps – two in the outer zone, one inside the camp itself.

Now look at this exam-style question relating to the text extract. **You don't need to answer it.** Instead, answer Question 1 below.

Component 1

Read lines 1–6.

A1. List **five** reasons why the labour camp is an unpleasant place. **(5 marks)**

To identify implicit ideas you need to read between the lines and think about what the writer is suggesting or implying. Explicit ideas are not hidden – you just need to find short quotations or paraphrase what is already in the text.

Guided

1 Read one student's answer to Question A1. For each point, decide whether the information is explicit or implicit.

The hammer is used to wake them up.	(Explicit) / Implicit
They have to get up at five o'clock.	Explicit / Implicit
The windows are covered with thick ice.	(Explicit) / Implicit
The sun is not yet up.	Explicit / Implicit
It is very cold.	Explicit / (Implicit)

Now read this extract, also from *One Day in the Life of Ivan Denisovich*, then answer Question 2.

He didn't get up. He lay there in his bunk on the top tier, his head buried in a blanket and a coat, his two feet stuffed into one sleeve, with the end tucked under, of his wadded jacket. He couldn't see, but his ears told him everything going on in the barrack-room and especially in the corner his team occupied. He heard the heavy tread of the orderlies carrying one of the big barrels of nightsoil along the passage outside. A light job, that was considered, a job for the infirm, but just you try and carry out the muck without spilling any. He heard some of the 75th slamming bunches of boots on to the floor from the drying-shed. Now their own lads were doing it (it was their own team's turn, too, to dry valenki). Tiurin, the team-leader, and his deputy Pavlo put on their valenki, without a word but he heard their bunks creaking.

2 Find four implicit ideas in the extract above that suggest that life in the labour camp is unpleasant.

(a) ....

(b) ....

(c) ....

(d) ....

Short questions on explicit and implicit information are only worth one mark for each point you make, so keep your answers brief. You don't always need to use quotations – you can also use your own words.

Had a go ☐ Nearly there ☐ Nailed it! ☐

Inference

Read this short extract from *To Kill a Mockingbird*, then answer Questions 1 and 2 below.

> I didn't look any more than I had to. Jem re-opened *Ivanhoe* and began reading. I tried to keep up with him, but he read too fast. When Jem came to a word he didn't know, he skipped it, but Mrs Dubose would catch him and make him spell it out. Jem read for perhaps twenty minutes, during which time I looked at the soot-stained mantelpiece, out of the window, anywhere to keep from looking at her.

1 Highlight or underline any phrases in the extract above that suggest the children dislike Mrs Dubose.

Guided

2 What impression of Mrs Dubose do you get from this short extract? Include two points, and use a short quotation to support each point and back up your answer.

When answering a question like this, think about what is suggested or implied about a character by the actions of other characters in the scene.

(a) The extract suggests that Mrs Dubose is ....

....

....

(b) ....

....

Now read this short extract, also from *To Kill a Mockingbird*, then answer Question 3 below.

> The following Monday afternoon Jem and I climbed the steep front steps to Mrs Dubose's house and padded down the open hallway. Jem, armed with *Ivanhoe* and full of superior knowledge, knocked at the second door on the left.
>
> 'Mrs Dubose?' he called.
>
> Jessie opened the wood door and unlatched the screen door.
>
> 'Is that you, Jem Finch?' she said. 'You got your sister with you. I don't know –'
>
> 'Let 'em both in, Jessie,' said Mrs Dubose. Jessie admitted us and went off to the kitchen.
>
> An oppressive odour met us when we crossed the threshold, an odour I had met many times in rain-rotted grey houses where there are coal-oil lamps, water dippers, and unbleached domestic sheets. It always made me afraid, expectant, watchful.
>
> In the corner of the room was a brass bed, and in the bed was Mrs Dubose. I wondered if Jem's activities had put her there, and for a moment I felt sorry for her. She was lying under a pile of quilts and looked almost friendly.
>
> There was a marble-topped washstand by her bed; on it were a glass with a teaspoon in it, a red ear syringe, a box of absorbent cotton, and a steel alarm clock standing on three tiny legs.
>
> 'So you brought that dirty little sister of yours, did you?' was her greeting.
>
> Jem said quietly, 'My sister ain't dirty and I ain't scared of you,' although I noticed his knees shaking.

Guided

3 Write about your impressions of Mrs Dubose and her house.

Mrs Dubose's house seems intimidating from the start of the extract, as it has 'steep front steps'. The house also frightens the children as they are met by an 'oppressive odour', which makes the narrator 'afraid, expectant' and 'watchful'. The odour is described as something usually smelt in 'rain-rotted' houses, which gives the reader the impression that the house

....

....

....

Interpreting information and ideas

Read this short extract from 'Occupations Accessible to Women', then answer Questions 1 and 2.

> Some hard study would, in some cases, be needed to supply the inaccuracy of the general style of a woman's knowledge as a very thorough grounding in elementary subjects is needful. Very few, even the most highly-educated of women, can work a sum in fractions or proportion with rapidity, much less explain every step of the process so clearly as to bring it within the comprehension of a class; and how few who write good English from habit can teach the rules of grammar correctly.
>
> The school selected should be taught by a very good certificated master or mistress, where an assistant should be likely to learn the system of school drill and discipline, and also how practically to manage children en masse, according to the latest approved Government rules.

Guided

1 Look at the words and phrases that have been underlined in the extract above and explain their meaning in your own words. The first two have been done for you.

(a) 'thorough grounding' *Good experience of, or background in*

(b) 'with rapidity' *With speed, or quickly*

(c) 'comprehension of a class' ....

(d) 'certificated' ....

(e) 'school drill' ....

Try reading the text before and after the word or phrase you need to explain. This may help you to infer the meaning.

2 Answer this exam-style question:

Component 2

A3. (a) What does the writer mean by 'manage children en masse'? **(1 mark)**

....

3 Now read this short extract, also from 'Occupations Accessible to Women', then answer the exam-style question that follows.

> THE great difficulty of the educational question in the present day, and the obstacle to complete success in the earnest efforts made, is the difficulty, almost impossibility, of finding sufficiently-qualified teachers. The demand created by the Education Acts is estimated at over 25,000 of both sexes – the women, however, being in the majority.

Component 2

A3. (a) What does the writer mean by 'earnest efforts made'? **(1 mark)**

(b) What does the writer feel is the main educational problem of the time? **(2 marks)**

(a) ....

(b) ....

....

Always look at how many marks are available for a question or question part. The question parts above are each worth only 1 or 2 marks, so keep your answers very brief.

Had a go ☐ Nearly there ☐ Nailed it! ☐

Point – Evidence – Explanation

Read this short extract from 'OK, you try teaching 13-year-olds', then answer the questions that follow.

> Shocking news: a young trainee languages teacher on placement at Tarleton High in Lancashire "lost it" in class, barricaded the door with furniture, trapping the pupils, and threatened to kill them with something nasty that she had in her handbag. But why shocking? Imagine yourself in her place, "teaching" about 30 13- or 14-year-old creatures. Do you have one or two in your house? Are they polite, quiet and cooperative? Or are they breathtakingly insolent, noisy, crabby, offensive, skulking, smoking, drugging, and whingeing that they are not suitably entertained? What if you had 30? Wouldn't you like something in your handbag to shut the little toads up?

1 The point below could be used to comment on the writer's use of language and its effect on the reader. Which piece of evidence below (A or B) most effectively supports this point? Circle your choice.

Point: The writer uses lists of adjectives to emphasise how difficult it can be to deal with teenagers.

Evidence A: 'whingeing that they are not suitably entertained'

Evidence B: 'insolent, noisy, crabby, offensive, ...'

2 Explain why the evidence you have chosen is the most effective for supporting the above point.

....

....

Guided

3 Select effective evidence from the extract to support the point below. Then choose the most effective explanation from the options given. Circle your choice.

Point: The writer uses strong verbs to emphasise the shocking nature of the teacher's actions.

Evidence: For example, she uses the words ....

....

Explanation A: These verbs emphasise how badly the teacher treated the children.

Explanation B: These verbs suggest that the teacher treated the children like prisoners. They also give the impression that she had completely lost her ability to manage the class and that she literally wanted to cause them harm.

4 Write one or two sentences, describing why your choice of explanation is more effective.

....

....

Point–Evidence–Explanation, or P-E-E, is particularly useful if you are asked to comment on language and structure, or to evaluate or compare a text. Improve your P-E-E paragraphs by using more than one piece of evidence to support a fully developed point.

Putting it into practice

Read the full extract from *The Day of the Triffids* on page 98, then answer the exam-style question below.

Component 1

Read lines 1–5.

A1. List **five** reasons why the triffids have not previously been seen as dangerous. **(5 marks)**

1 (a) ....

(b) ....

(c) ....

(d) ....

(e) ....

2 Now write two P-E-E paragraphs of an answer to the exam-style question below.

When you tackle this kind of question in the exam, remember to:

- spend about 12 minutes on your answer
- identify the main focus of the question
- read the text carefully and annotate it with your ideas
- only use the lines of the extract referred to in the question
- comment on how the writer uses language and structure and what the effects are on the reader.

Component 1

Read lines 18–30.

A3. What impression do you get of the early reactions to the triffids from these lines? **(10 marks)**

You must refer to the text to support your answer.

....

....

....

....

....

....

....

....

....

....

Remember: You are only being asked to write part of an answer on this page. In the exam, where you will write a full answer, you will have more space for your answer.

Had a go ☐ Nearly there ☐ Nailed it! ☐

Putting it into practice

Read the full extract from 'OK, you try teaching 13-year-olds' on page 103.

1 Write three P-E-E paragraphs of an answer to the exam-style question below.

When you tackle this kind of question in the exam, remember to:

- spend about 12 minutes on your answer
- identify the main focus of the question
- read the text carefully and annotate it with your ideas
- only use the lines of the extract referred to in the question
- comment on how the writer uses language and structure and what the effects are on the reader.

Component 

A2. Michele Hanson is trying to show us how difficult it is to be a teacher. How does she try to do this? **(10 marks)**

You should write about:

- what she says to influence readers
- her use of language and tone
- the way she presents her argument.

Remember: You are only being asked to write part of an answer on this page. In the exam, where you will write a full answer, you will have more space for your answer.

Word classes

Read this short extract from 'OK, you try teaching 13-year-olds', then answer Questions 1 and 2.

> Shocking news: a young trainee languages teacher on placement at Tarleton High in Lancashire "lost it" in class, (barricaded) the door with furniture, trapping the pupils, and threatened to kill them with something nasty that she had in her handbag. But why shocking? Imagine yourself in her place, "teaching" about 30 13- or 14-year-old creatures. Do you have one or two in your house? Are they polite, quiet and cooperative? Or are they (breathtakingly) insolent, noisy, crabby, offensive, skulking, smoking, drugging, and whingeing that they are not suitably entertained?

Verb

Adverb

Guided

1 Circle and label at least one example of each of the following word classes. Two have been done for you:

- noun
- verb
- adverb
- adjective.

> Remember that adjectives can become comparatives (e.g. noisier, more insolent) and superlatives (e.g. noisiest, most insolent).

2 The writer uses lists of adjectives in her rhetorical questions about teenagers. What effect do these lists of adjectives have on the reader?

....

....

....

....

....

Now read this short extract from *One Day in the Life of Ivan Denisovich*, then answer Question 3.

> Shukhov remembered that this morning his fate hung in the balance: they wanted to shift the 104th from the building-shops to a new site, the "Socialist Way of Life" settlement. It lay in open country covered with snowdrifts, and before anything else could be done there they would have to dig pits and put up posts and attach barbed wire to them. Wire themselves in, so that they wouldn't run away. Only then would they start building.

3 In this extract, the writer uses action verbs to emphasise how harsh life is in the labour camp. Identify two examples of action verbs and explain their effects on the reader.

(a) ....

....

....

(b) ....

....

....

Had a go ☐ Nearly there ☐ Nailed it! ☐

Connotations

Read this short extract from *The Boys Are Back in Town*, then answer Question 1.

It is what I like to think of as a masculine quality, the theory of outer markers. The boys have very definite limits that they mustn't go beyond. Inside the perimeter they can do very much as they please, but they must stay inside the boundaries. It's murky on the other side, they're frightened of the dark out there, I've had to see to that. But within the limits it's summertime and it's easy living.

1 (a) Draw lines to match the circled words or phrases to their possible connotations.

outer markers   perimeter   boundaries

border   sport   outer space   outskirts   extreme edge   dividing line   cricket pitch   limits

Words can have different meanings depending on their context – what comes before and after them in a text. Thinking about the context of a word will help you to understand its connotations.

(b) What ideas and attitudes about parenting do the circled words or phrases suggest to the reader?

....

....

....

Now read this short extract from *To Kill a Mockingbird*, then answer Question 2.

The following Monday afternoon Jem and I climbed the steep front steps to Mrs Dubose's house and padded down the open hallway. Jem, armed with *Ivanhoe* and full of superior knowledge, knocked at the second door on the left.

'Mrs Dubose?' he called.

Jessie opened the wood door and unlatched the screen door.

'Is that you, Jem Finch?' she said. 'You got your sister with you. I don't know –'

'Let 'em both in, Jessie,' said Mrs Dubose. Jessie admitted us and went off to the kitchen.

An oppressive odour met us when we crossed the threshold, an odour I had met many times in rain-rotted grey houses where there are coal-oil lamps, water dippers, and unbleached domestic sheets.

2 Circle two words or phrases from the extract above. Write a sentence commenting on the connotations of each one.

(a) ....

....

....

(b) ....

....

....

Figurative language

Read this short extract from *To Kill a Mockingbird*, then answer Question 1.

> She was horrible. Her face was the colour of a dirty pillowcase, and the corners of her mouth glistened with wet, which inched like a glacier down the deep grooves enclosing her chin. Old-age liver spots dotted her cheeks, and her pale eyes had black pinpoint pupils. Her hands were knobby, and the cuticles were grown up over her fingernails. Her bottom plate was not in, and her upper lip protruded; from time to time she would draw her nether lip to her upper plate and carry her chin with it. This made the wet move faster.

Guided

1 The writer uses the word 'glacier' figuratively. What does this simile suggest to the reader about Mrs Dubose?

The writer uses the simile 'like a glacier', which has connotations of ....

....

This suggests to the reader ....

....

....

Now read this short extract, also from *To Kill a Mockingbird*, then answer Questions 2 and 3.

> From time to time she would open her mouth wide, and I could see her tongue undulate faintly. Cords of saliva would collect on her lips; she would draw them in, then open her mouth again. Her mouth seemed to have a private existence of its own. It worked separate and apart from the rest of her, out and in, like a clam hole at low tide. Occasionally it would say, 'Pt,' like some viscous substance coming to a boil.

Don't just identify and name a figurative device used in a text. Remember to comment on the effect the device has on the reader.

2 Identify at least one simile from the extract above. Write one or two sentences commenting on why the writer has used it and its effect on the reader.

....

....

....

3 Identify the metaphor the writer has used in the extract above. (Hint: look closely at the second sentence.) Write a P-E-E paragraph explaining why the writer has used it and its effect on the reader.

....

....

....

....

Creation of character

Read this short extract from *To Kill a Mockingbird*, then answer Question 1.

> 'So you brought that dirty little sister of yours, did you?' was her greeting.
>
> Jem said quietly, 'My sister ain't dirty and I ain't scared of you,' although I noticed his knees shaking.
>
> I was expecting a tirade, but all she said was, 'You may commence reading, Jeremy.'

Guided

1 In the extract above, the writer uses dialogue to create ideas about the characters. What ideas does this use of dialogue give the reader about both Mrs Dubose and Jem?

The writer uses dialogue to show that Mrs Dubose is rude as she calls Jem's sister 'dirty'. However, Jem's dialogue shows that he is ....

....

....

....

....

Now read this short extract, also from *To Kill a Mockingbird*, then answer Question 2.

> I didn't look any more than I had to. Jem re-opened *Ivanhoe* and began reading. I tried to keep up with him, but he read too fast. When Jem came to a word he didn't know, he skipped it, but Mrs Dubose would catch him and make him spell it out. Jem read for perhaps twenty minutes, during which time I looked at the soot-stained mantelpiece, out of the window, anywhere to keep from looking at her. As he read along, I noticed that Mrs Dubose's corrections grew fewer and farther between, that Jem had even left one sentence dangling in mid-air. She was not listening.

2 How do Jem's actions in the extract above build up an idea of his character?

....

....

....

Turn to the full extract from *To Kill a Mockingbird* on page 97. Read lines 22–39, focusing on the description of Mrs Dubose. Then answer Question 3.

Character can be created through dialogue, description or action.

3 Write a P-E-E paragraph about how the writer creates ideas about the character of Mrs Dubose.

....

....

....

....

....

....

Creating atmosphere

Read this short extract from *Enduring Love,* then answer Questions 1 to 3.

> The wind renewed its (rage) in the treetops just before I felt its (force) on my back. Then it (struck) the balloon which ceased its innocent comical wagging and was suddenly stilled. Its only motion was a shimmer of strain that rippled out across its ridged surface as the contained energy accumulated. It broke free, the anchor flew up in a spray of dirt, and the balloon and basket rose ten feet in the air. The boy was thrown back, out of sight. The pilot had the rope in his hands and was lifted two feet clear off the ground. If Logan had not reached him and taken hold of one of the many dangling lines the balloon would have carried the boy away. Instead, both men were now being pulled across the field, and the farm workers and I were running again.

1 What are the connotations of the words circled in the extract above?

'rage' ....

'force' ....

'struck' ....

2 Look at the first half of the extract above, up to the words 'rose ten feet in the air'. Find and circle examples of the following: action verbs, personification, adjectives.

3 In the answer extracts below, students have commented on the atmosphere in the first half of the extract from *Enduring Love*. They have used their answers to Questions 1 and 2 in their writing.

A

> A tense atmosphere is created by the writer using the word 'rage'. This suggests the wind is angry.

B

> The writer creates a tense atmosphere by personifying the wind. It is said to be in a 'rage' and to create a 'force'. This suggests that it is actually fighting the narrator and this is emphasised by use of the action verb 'struck'.

C

> The atmosphere is tense. This is shown by the use of personification of the wind and by the use of strong verbs like 'struck' and 'broke'.
>
> The writer also uses adjectives to show the wind is strong, like 'rippled' and 'ridged'.

(a) Circle the answer extract you think is most effective (A, B or C).

(b) Explain why you feel your chosen answer extract is the most effective.

....

....

....

Read the second half of the extract from *Enduring Love* above, from the words 'The boy was thrown back' to '...were running again'. Then answer Question 4.

> When you answer a question about language techniques in the exam, start with an overview to summarise the overall effect of the extract.

Guided

4 Using your answers to Questions 1 to 3, write an overview sentence that sums up the overall atmosphere created in the extract at the top of this page.

Overall, the writer creates an atmosphere of ....

....

....

Narrative voice

Read extracts 1, 2 and 3 below.

Extract 1: from *Enduring Love*

> I should make something clear. There may have been a vague communality of purpose, but we were never a team. There was no chance, no time. Coincidences of time and place, a predisposition to help had brought us together under the balloon. No one was in charge – or everyone was, and we were in a shouting match. The pilot, red-faced, bawling and sweating, we ignored. Incompetence came off him like heat. But we were beginning to bawl our own instructions too. I know that if I had been uncontested leader the tragedy would not have happened.

Extract 2: from *The Day of the Triffids*

> I woke up to find myself in bed, with my mother, my father, and the doctor watching me anxiously. My head felt as if it were split open, I was aching all over, and, as I later discovered, one side of my face was decorated with a blotchy-red raised weal. The insistent questions as to how I came to be lying unconscious in the garden were quite useless; I had no faintest idea what it was that had hit me.

Extract 3: from *One Day in the Life of Ivan Denisovich*

> Shukhov never overslept reveille. He always got up at once, for the next ninety minutes, until they assembled for work, belonged to him, not to the authorities, and any old-timer could always earn a bit–by sewing a pair of over-mittens for someone out of old sleeve lining;

Now read the descriptions of narrative voice below, then answer Questions 1 and 2.

A

First-person narrative has been used to allow the reader to know the narrator's feelings about the other characters.

B

Third-person narrative has been used. This 'omniscient narrator' knows everything, including the narrator's feelings and motives.

C

First-person narrative has been used to keep some of the details from the reader. This increases the tension.

1 Match each extract (1, 2, 3) above to one of the descriptions of narrative voice (A, B, C). Write the letters of the descriptions in the spaces below to make the matches.

Extract 1: ....

Extract 2: ....

Extract 3: ....

Narrative voice is the 'voice' a writer of fiction chooses to tell the story. A writer can choose a narrative voice to create a particular point of view.

2 Re-read Extract 1. How has the first person narrative voice been used to suggest that the main character views himself as the most effective of the rescuers?

....

....

....

Putting it into practice

1 Read the full extract from *Enduring Love* on page 99, then answer the exam-style question below.

Component ①

Read lines 1–14.

A4. How does the writer create a sense of drama and tension in these lines? **(10 marks)**

You should write about:

- what happens to build drama and tension
- the writer's use of language to create drama and tension
- the effects on the reader.

When you tackle this type of question in the exam, remember to:

- spend around 12 minutes on your answer
- read the question carefully and highlight the main focus
- read the source text thoroughly, annotating as you read
- only use the lines of the text referred to in the question
- identify the language and structural devices used and comment on their effects
- support all your points with clear evidence and a clear explanation by using a P-E-E structure in your paragraphs.

In the exam you will need to write about structure to answer this kind of question. Structure is covered later in this Workbook. Here, you just need to comment on how the writer uses language – skills you have covered on pages 17–22.

Remember: You have more space than this to answer your question in the exam. Use your own paper to finish your answer to the question above.

Putting it into practice

1 Answer the exam-style question.

Read lines 34–41.

A3. What impression do you get of life in the labour camp from these lines? **(10 marks)**

You must refer to the text to support your answer.

When you tackle this type of question in the exam, remember to:

- spend around 12 minutes on your answer
- read the question carefully and highlight the main focus
- read the source text thoroughly, annotating as you read
- only use the lines of the text referred to in the question
- identify the language and structural devices used and comment on their effects
- support all your points with clear evidence and a clear explanation by using a P-E-E structure in your paragraphs.

Remember: You have more space than this to answer your question in the exam. Use your own paper to finish your answer to the question above.

Rhetorical devices 1

Read this short extract from 'OK, you try teaching 13-year-olds', then answer Questions 1 and 2.

Shocking news: a young trainee languages teacher on placement at Tarleton High in Lancashire "lost it" in class, barricaded the door with furniture, trapping the pupils, and threatened to kill them with something nasty that she had in her handbag. But why shocking? Imagine yourself in her place, "teaching" about 30 13- or 14-year-old creatures. Do you have one or two in your house? Are they polite, quiet and cooperative? Or are they breathtakingly insolent, noisy, crabby, offensive, skulking, smoking, drugging, and whingeing that they are not suitably entertained? What if you had 30? Wouldn't you like something in your handbag to shut the little toads up?

1 Find four of the following rhetorical devices in the extract above. Circle them below and label them in the extract.

- pattern of three
- lists
- alliteration
- rhetorical questions
- colloquial language

Guided

2 For each device you have identified, write one or two sentences commenting on:

- why the writer has used it
- the intended effect on the reader.

The answer has been started for you, with comments about the writer's use of lists.

Remember to think about how rhetorical devices are used by considering their effect on the reader.

The writer uses a list of negative adjectives, such as 'insolent, noisy' and 'crabby' to emphasise how difficult teenagers can be. As this list comes after the description of the teacher's actions, it might make readers feel some sympathy for teachers. The writer also uses ....

....

....

....

....

....

....

....

....

....

....

....

....

Had a go ☐ Nearly there ☐ Nailed it! ☐

Rhetorical devices 2

Read this short extract from *The Boys Are Back in Town* by Simon Carr, then answer Question 1.

> Mothers tend to a different theory. They take a more active interest in the details and the way stations through the day. Mothers like a routine; they even say that children like a routine ('It gives them security'). The bath before bedtime calms them down. This may be true, too, but in our house there aren't bedtimes, let alone baths before them.

1 The writer has a very relaxed attitude to parenting. How does the repetition of 'Mothers' and 'routine' help to show this attitude?

....

....

....

Now read the first three sentences of the next paragraph from *The Boys Are Back in Town*, up to the words 'they drive you nuts'. Then answer Question 2.

> The canon law my boys operate to is listed here in no particular order. No interrupting adults. Of course we like talking to children and we like them talking to us, but those demands for food, drink or attention that come in from nowhere, unasked, unexpected, they drive you nuts. Yes, and no swearing if you're a child not even words that sound like swearing. Except damn, of course, and hell. What else? As little stealing and lying as possible. No wanton littering, no fighting except for fun or out of earshot. Be polite as much as possible – of course, you can't when you're very angry. *You must work hard at school.* Screaming insanely, running round the house making absurd and disgusting noises, sliding in the mud in the park after dark and throwing water bombs and tennis balls at windows – all these were encouraged.

2 The underlined section in the extract above provides a contrast (an opposing or different idea) to the ideas mothers have about parenting in the first extract on this page. Write one or two sentences explaining how this use of contrast helps to demonstrate the writer's relaxed attitude to his children.

....

....

....

Read the rest of the extract from *The Boys Are Back in Town* above, from the words 'Yes, and no swearing' to 'all these were encouraged'. Then answer Question 3.

> If you know it, use the technical name for the device in your answer. If you don't know the technical name, you should still comment on the language and its effect.

3 Identify one example of hyperbole and one example of emotive language in the second extract above. Write one or two sentences commenting on why the writer has used each rhetorical device and the effect each one has on the reader.

Hyperbole: ....

....

Emotive language: ....

....

Fact, opinion and expert evidence

Read the following three quotations from an article about teaching, then answer Question 1.

A In 2013, almost 50,000 teachers gave up teaching.

B Research from the Department for Education suggests that difficult working conditions are the main cause.

C Teaching is the most rewarding of all professions.

1 Identify which of the above extracts is:

(a) a fact ....

(b) an opinion ....

(c) expert evidence ....

Think about how the fact, opinion or expert evidence helps to support the writer's viewpoint or argument.

Now read the short extract from 'OK, you try teaching 13-year-olds' below. Then answer Questions 2 to 4.

> I'm trying not to sound bitter here, but I have taught; I have known supply-teaching hell; and I, too, have blown my top, even though it was 3.30pm and nearly over, because by then they were still climbing up walls (really), throwing scissors, dribbling glue and screaming all the while … and when that happens, sometimes one just cannot keep one's cool a second longer.
>
> And 13 is a particularly cruel age. In my first year's teaching, I crashed the car and sliced my forehead open on the sun-visor. Back at school, with my unsightly 27-stitch scar, I passed two 13-year-old girls. "She looks uglier than ever," said they, laughing merrily.

2 Write one sentence summing up the writer's viewpoint in the extract above.

....

....

3 Identify at least one fact, one opinion and one piece of expert evidence the writer uses to support her viewpoint. Highlight or underline these in the extract above.

4 Write a sentence for each example you have identified in Question 3, explaining how it supports the writer's viewpoint.

Remember that the person providing the expert evidence could be the author of the text, as in this case!

Fact: ....

....

Opinion: ....

....

Expert evidence: ....

....

Identifying sentence types

Look at the sentences below, then answer the questions that follow.

A My hands were trembling.

B Even though I had done this hundreds of times before, I was still terrified.

C My blood ran cold and my heart stopped.

D Blind terror.

1 Look carefully at the four sentences above. Each one is a different type of sentence. But which is which?

Sentence .... is a single-clause sentence.

Sentence .... is a multi-clause sentence (coordinate).

Sentence .... is a multi-clause sentence (subordinate).

Sentence .... is a minor sentence.

Now read this short extract from 'OK, you try teaching 13-year-olds', then answer Question **2**.

> Now think of that young teacher. "She had been trying to get them to be quiet," we learn. So she had probably been shouted at and humiliated for 40 minutes. This was her very last day of several horrible weeks of a placement. The end of her torment was a whisker away, but, driven barmy by pupils, she still blew it. Her career is now ruined. But the children were "petrified … burst into tears" and were offered "support". The pathetic little wets. She was pretending, you fools – dredging up a last desperate ploy to shut the monsters up. If she had cried, they would have laughed out loud. Hopefully, she won't be sacked. If that's what she really, really wants.

2 In the extract above, highlight or circle one example of each kind of sentence: single-clause, multi-clause (subordinate), multi-clause (coordinate) and minor.

> SINGLE-CLAUSE sentences are made up of just **one clause** and provide **one piece of information** about an event or action. They contain **a subject** and **one verb**.
> MULTI-CLAUSE sentences are made up of **more than one claus**e. They contain **two or more verbs**.
> SUBORDINATE clauses do not make sense on their own. They are **dependent** on the main clause.
> COORDINATE clauses are an **equal pair**, where neither clause is dependent on the other.
> MINOR SENTENCES are grammatically incomplete because they **do not contain a verb**.

Commenting on sentence types

Read this short extract from ''Appy ever after', then answer Question 1.

> He hands me the controller. I select Calm mode. I turn the dial up and – *Holy silicon mad professors!* – it hurts. There's a sharp vibration that feels like the neurons in my head are pogoing. Not relaxing at all. I turn it down and wait. And then something remarkable happens. After a few minutes, I begin to feel waves gently flowing through my head. I don't notice at first but soon I begin to slump in my chair, my pupils dilate and my breathing slows.

1 The extract above starts with short single-clause sentences and ends with a long, multi-clause sentence that has several subordinate clauses. How do these sentence structures suggest what is happening to the narrator's feelings?

....

....

....

....

....

Now read this short extract from *Enduring Love*, then answer Question 2.

> I got there before them. When I took a rope the basket was above head height. The boy inside it was screaming. Despite the wind, I caught the smell of urine. Jed Parry was on a rope seconds after me and the two farm workers, Joseph Lacey and Toby Greene, caught hold just after him. Greene was having a coughing fit, but he kept his grip. The pilot was shouting instructions at us, but too frantically, and no one was listening.

Guided

2 In this extract, the writer uses a variety of sentence lengths to create a sense of tension. Explain how the sentence structures create tension.

The writer starts the paragraph with a short, single-clause sentence ....

....

....

....

After using short sentences, the writer then uses a multi-clause sentence. This adds to the tension ....

....

....

....

The writer then uses two multi-clause sentences that end with subordinate clauses. This adds to the tension ....

....

....

....

Had a go ☐ Nearly there ☐ Nailed it! ☐

Structure: non-fiction

Read this short extract from 'OK, you try teaching 13-year-olds' by Michele Hanson, then answer Question 1.

> Shocking news: a young trainee languages teacher on placement at Tarleton High in Lancashire "lost it" in class, barricaded the door with furniture, trapping the pupils, and threatened to kill them with something nasty that she had in her handbag.

1 The opening of any text needs to engage the reader. In the extract above, the writer chooses to use the opening to set the scene. How has she ensured that readers will want to read on?

....

....

Now read the full extract from 'OK, you try teaching 13-year-olds' on page 103. Then answer Question 2.

2 Consider the following ways in which writers can end their writing in order to leave a lasting impression:

vivid images | warnings | calls to action | positivity | summary of main points made

Circle the one you think most suits the way Michele Hanson ends her article and explain why you think she chose to end it that way.

....

....

Read this short extract from the article ''Appy ever after' by John Arlidge:

> The trouble is, Goldwasser has just attached two electrodes to my head and is about to start pumping electricity straight into my brain.

Now read this second short extract, from later in the same article, before answering Question 3. The electricity is now flowing through the electrodes into Arlidge's head:

> And then something remarkable happens. After a few minutes I begin to feel waves gently flowing through my head. I don't notice at first but soon I begin to slump in my chair, my pupils dilate and my breathing slows.

Guided

3 Writers need to keep the interest of their readers and they often do it by changing the tone in the middle section of their writing. How does Arlidge do this in the extracts from his article above?

Initially, Arlidge is scared about the idea of having two electrodes attached to his head. This is implied in the phrase 'pumping electricity straight into my brain'. However, when he actually tries the electrodes, his tone changes ....

....

....

....

Structure: fiction

Read the full extract from *Enduring Love* on page 99. Now focus on these lines from the extract, before answering Questions 1 and 2:

> What we saw when we stood from our picnic was this: a huge grey balloon, the size of a house, the shape of a tear drop, had come down in the field. The pilot must have been half way out of the passenger basket as it touched the ground. His leg had become entangled in a rope that was attached to an anchor. Now, as the wind gusted, and pushed and lifted the balloon towards the escarpment, he was being half dragged, half carried across the field. In the basket was a child, a boy of about ten.

1 How do the sentences underlined in the short extract above foreshadow the drama that follows later in the extract?

. . . .

. . . .

Guided **2** In the extract above, why does the writer leave the information about the boy in the basket until after he has written about the wind?

The writer withholds the fact that there is a boy in the basket as this structure increases the tension for the reader. Before this fact is revealed, the writer closely describes . . . .

. . . .

. . . .

The revelation that there is a boy in the basket increases the tension because . . . .

. . . .

. . . .

Now focus on what happens next in the extract, before answering Question 3:

> In a sudden lull, the man was on his feet, clutching at the basket, or at the boy. Then there was another gust, and the pilot was on his back, bumping over the rough ground, trying to dig his feet in for purchase, or lunging for the anchor behind him in order to secure it in the earth. Even if he had been able, he would not have dared disentangle himself from the anchor rope. He needed his weight to keep the balloon on the ground, and the wind could have snatched the rope from his hands.

3 Here, the writer describes the actions of the man and what happens to the balloon in great detail. What is the effect of this structure on the reader?

. . . .

. . . .

. . . .

. . . .

> Remember that writers of fiction use a variety of narrative structures for effect. These include foreshadowing, use of closely described detail or action, repetition and dialogue.

Putting it into practice

1 Read the full extract from *The Day of the Triffids* on page 98, then answer the exam-style question below.

Component 1

Read lines 40–55.

A4. How does the writer increase the tension in these lines? **(10 marks)**

You should write about:

- what happens to increase the tension
- the writer's use of language to create tension
- the effects on the reader.

When you tackle this type of question in the exam, remember to:

- spend around 12 minutes on your answer
- read the question carefully and highlight the main focus
- read the source text thoroughly, annotating as you read
- only use the lines of the text referred to in the question
- identify the language and structural devices used and comment on their effects.

In the exam you will also need to write about language to answer this kind of question. You practised this on page 23 of this Workbook. Here, however, just practise commenting on how the writer uses sentences and structure – skills you have covered on pages 28, 29 and 31.

Remember: You have more space than this to answer your question in the exam. Use your own paper to finish your answer to the question above.

Putting it into practice

1 Read the full extract from ''Appy ever after' on page 101, then answer the exam-style question below.

Component 

A2. John Arlidge is trying to engage the reader by explaining mood-altering techniques. How does he try to do this? **(10 marks)**

You should comment on:

- what he says to entertain the readers
- his use of language and tone
- the way he presents his argument.

When you tackle this type of question in the exam, remember to:

- spend around 12 minutes on your answer
- read the question carefully and highlight the main focus
- read the source text thoroughly, annotating as you read
- identify the language and structural devices used and comment on their effects.

Remember: You have more space than this to answer your question in the exam. Use your own paper to finish your answer to the question above.

Had a go ☐ Nearly there ☐ Nailed it! ☐

Handling two texts

In Component 2, two assessment objectives will test your ability to handle two texts together. These are Assessment objectives 1 (b) and 3. Read the assessment objectives, then answer Questions 1 and 2.

Assessment objective 1 (b)
Select and synthesise evidence from different texts

Assessment objective 3
Compare writers' ideas and perspectives, as well as how these are conveyed, across two or more texts

1 Circle the word below which is **not** a synonym for 'synthesise'.

combine | fuse | amalgamate | blend | mix | separate

The texts in Component 2 may be similar or different in various ways. Think about:
- the ideas they express about the topic
- the language they use
- their points of view
- how they are structured.

2 Which of the assessment objectives above will require you to identify **and** explain both similarities **and** differences between the two texts? ....

Now look at these exam-style questions. **You don't need to answer these questions.** Instead, think about how they test the skills in Assessment objectives 1 (b) and 3 and then answer Question 3.

To answer the following questions you will need to use both texts.

A5. According to these two writers, what are the rules for mothers when bringing up their children? **(4 marks)**

A6. Both of these texts are about parenting. Compare:
- the writers' attitudes to parenting
- the ways in which they get across their points about parenting. **(10 marks)**

You must use the text to support your comments and make it clear which text you are referring to.

3 Read the statements below. Decide which component or question each statement describes. Circle your choices.

(a) The two non-fiction texts will always be linked by a common theme or topic, so they will always have something in common. **Component 1 Component 2**

(b) This question will test Assessment objective 3 by asking you to compare the texts. **Question A5 Question A6**

(c) This question will test Assessment objective 1 (b) by asking you to synthesise information from both texts. **Question A5 Question A6**

(d) This question is worth only 4 marks, so you should only make about two or three points. **Question A5 Question A6**

(e) This question is worth 10 marks, so you should spend more time on this question. **Question A5 Question A6**

(f) For this question, you will need to compare the language used as well as looking at the writers' attitudes and ideas. **Question A5 Question A6**

(g) For this question, you should start by giving an overview to show your understanding of the question. **Question A5 Question A6**

Selecting evidence for synthesis

When selecting information for the synthesis question (A5 in Component 2), you need to choose evidence that is relevant to the question. Read the exam-style question below. **You don't need to answer this question.** Instead, think about what it is asking you to do, then answer Questions 1 and 2.

Component ②

To answer the following question you will need to use both texts.

A5. According to these two writers, what are the positive aspects of mind-altering techniques? **(4 marks)**

1 Underline or highlight the key words in Question A5.

2 Look at the short extracts below. Which ones would be a good source of relevant quotations in answer to Question A5 above? Circle one extract from each text.

(a) Extracts from **''Appy ever after'**

i Goldwasser believes harnessing willpower will have big implications in the treatment of obesity, alcoholism or gambling addiction…

ii Thync is focusing on willpower, self-control, motivation, confidence and creativity.

(b) Extracts from **'Victorian Hypnotism'**

i Legs and breasts may be amputated, children born, teeth extracted, in short the most painful experiences undergone, with no other anæsthetic than the hypnotizer's assurance that no pain shall be felt. Similarly morbid pains may be annihilated, neuralgias, toothaches, rheumatisms cured.

ii Hallucinations and histrionic delusions generally go with a certain depth of the trance, and are followed by complete forgetfulness.

As only 4 marks are available for the synthesis question, skim read the texts to save time.

Now read the full extracts from *The Boys Are Back in Town* on page 100 and 'The Rearing and Management of Children' on page 105. Then read the exam-style question below. **You don't need to answer this question.** Instead, think about what it is asking you to do, then answer Question 3.

Component ②

To answer the following question you will need to use both texts.

A5. According to these two writers, what are the rules for mothers when bringing up children? **(4 marks)**

3 Both texts suggest that mothers follow strict rules and routines for bringing up children. Write out the evidence that supports this similarity.

. . . .

. . . .

. . . .

. . . .

Had a go ☐ Nearly there ☐ Nailed it! ☐

Synthesising evidence

When you are synthesising the evidence you have selected from the two non-fiction texts in Component 2, you need to use suitable adverbials and linking phrases. Answer Questions 1 and 2.

Guided

1 Tick or circle the adverbials and linking phrases below that are suitable for synthesising evidence. Two examples have been done for you.

similarly | on the other hand | (likewise) | both | in the same way | however | (also)

2 Why should you use adverbials and linking phrases in your synthesis of evidence?

....

....

To show your full understanding of the synthesis question, you should start your answer with an overview. Read the exam-style question below. **You don't need to answer this question now.** Instead, think about what it is asking you to do, then answer Question 3.

Component 2

To answer the following question you will need to use both texts.

A5. According to these two writers, what are the positive aspects of mind-altering techniques? **(4 marks)**

3 Look at the overviews below, which students have written in response to Question A5.

A Both writers write about mind-altering techniques.

B Both writers write about mind-altering techniques, one writes about hypnosis and the other about a mind-altering machine.

C Both writers feel that mind-altering techniques can have a positive impact on health and happiness.

(a) Tick or circle the overview that you think is most effective.

(b) Explain why the overview you have chosen would be the best way to start an answer to Question A5 above.

....

....

....

4 Read the full extracts from ''Appy ever after' by John Arlidge on page 101 and 'Victorian Hypnotism' on page 102. Then write one synthesis paragraph in answer to Question A5 above.

- Use suitable adverbials and linking phrases from the selection at the top of this page.
- Start your paragraph with the overview you chose for Question 3.
- You could use the evidence you identified on page 35.

Try to make each sentence cover both texts. Use short quotations where possible, or paraphrase the text if a quotation would be too long.

....

....

....

Looking closely at language

Read this short extract from ''Appy ever after', then answer Questions 1 to 3.

> Goldwasser and Tyler may sound bonkers, but if their timing is anything to go by, they're the smartest guys in the lab. Wearable gizmos are the hottest new sector in the trillion-pound global technology sector. Apple launches its first smartwatch in the new year and will be followed by wearable kit from Microsoft and Google, which promises new versions of its web-enabled spectacles, Google Glass. Many of the new devices are designed to improve our health by monitoring our blood pressure and our stress levels, keeping tabs on how much exercise we take and helping us to feel refreshed in the morning by waking us up as we are coming out of a period of deep sleep.

Guided

1 What are the connotations of the words and phrases circled in the extract above? The first one has been done for you.

'bonkers' This means 'mad', 'crazy' or 'wild'. It's an informal term so it could have positive connotations.

'gizmos' ....

'wearable kit' ....

2 Write one or two sentences explaining the effect created by the words and phrases circled in the extract. Use the words and phrases as quotations and make sure you refer to their connotations.

....

....

....

3 The final sentence (underlined in the extract above) is very long and has several subordinate clauses. How does this sentence change the tone of this short extract?

....

....

....

Now read this short extract, also from ''Appy ever after', then answer Question 4.

> Goldwasser and Tyler are taking the idea one step further, giving us the power to change the way we feel, whenever we want.
>
> "Tap into your self-control. Tap into your creativity. Tap into your energy. Tap into your calm. Think of us as your third cup of coffee in the morning or your glass of wine at night," Goldwasser smiles.

4 Look at the language and sentence structure in the extract above.

(a) Identify the rhetorical device used. Write a sentence commenting on the effect it creates.

....

....

(b) Explain the effect created by the sentence structure.

....

....

In Component 2, the final reading question will ask you to compare language across both non-fiction texts. Use the skills you have revised here but remember that you must not write about one text without making a comparison point about the other. Try to give the texts equal weighting in your answer.

Had a go ☐ Nearly there ☐ Nailed it! ☐

Planning to compare

Read the short extracts 1 and 2 below. Then answer Question 1.

Extract 1: from 'Occupations Accessible to Women'

The duties of teachers in elementary schools are both healthful and congenial. The hours of work vary in some schools according to the season of the year, but usually the children assemble at 9:30 a.m. and are dismissed at 4:30 p.m. A quarter of an hour's run is allowed them at eleven, and an hour and a quarter (sometimes more) for dinner, thus reducing the actual school hours to five hours and a half. After school the hours are free for recreation, pleasant visits, or study.

Extract 2: from 'OK, you try teaching 13-year-olds'

I'm trying not to sound bitter here, but I have taught; I have known supply-teaching hell; and I, too, have blown my top, even though it was 3.30pm and nearly over, because by then they were still climbing up walls (really), throwing scissors, dribbling glue and screaming all the while … and when that happens, sometimes one just cannot keep one's cool a second longer.

And 13 is a particularly cruel age. In my first year's teaching, I crashed the car and sliced my forehead open on the sun-visor. Back at school, with my unsightly 27-stitch scar, I passed two 13-year-old girls. "She looks uglier than ever," said they, laughing merrily.

Guided

1 Now look at one student's plan for comparing the language in the two texts, and its effects. The plan is incomplete. Add as many details as you can, for example, quotations and explanations.

When comparing you can:
- start with the language and structural techniques the texts have in common, then compare the effects created

OR
- start with similarities in the effects of the two texts (for example, tone), then compare the techniques the writers have used to create those effects.

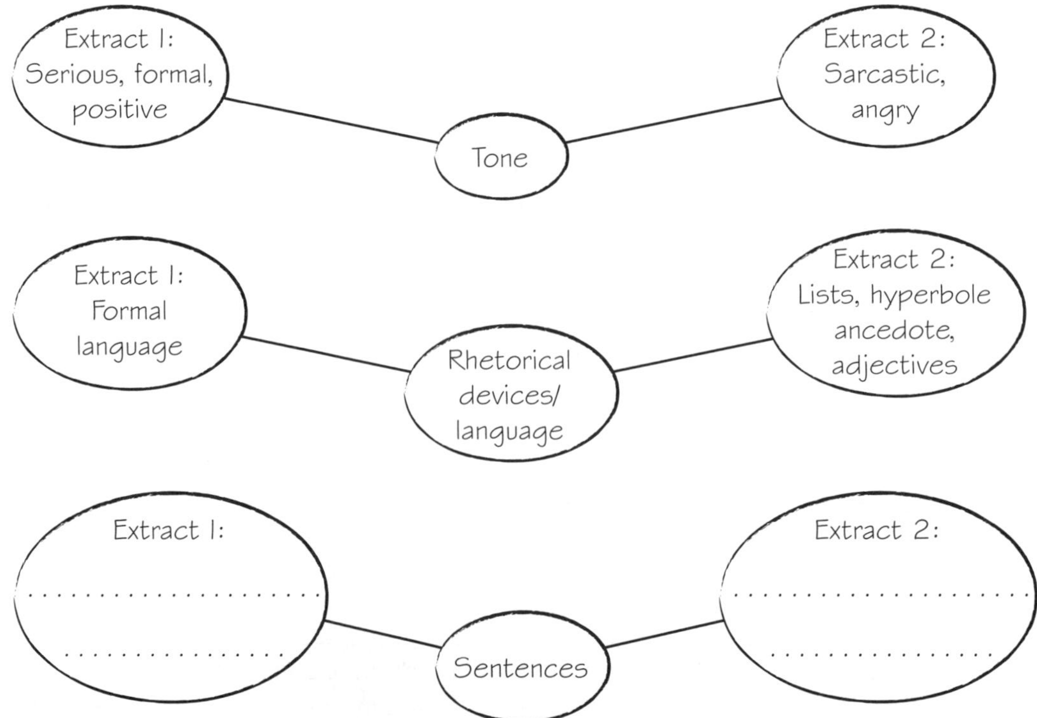

Comparing ideas

Read the openings of 'OK, you try teaching 13-year-olds' and 'Occupations Accessible to Women'.

Extract 1: 'OK, you try teaching 13-year-olds'

> Shocking news: a young trainee languages teacher on placement at Tarleton High in Lancashire "lost it" in class, barricaded the door with furniture, trapping the pupils, and threatened to kill them with something nasty that she had in her handbag. But why shocking? Imagine yourself in her place, "teaching" about 30 13- or 14-year-old creatures.

Extract 2: 'Occupations Accessible to Women'

> THE great difficulty of the educational question in the present day, and the obstacle to complete success in the earnest efforts made, is the difficulty, almost impossibility, of finding sufficiently-qualified teachers. The demand created by the Education Acts is estimated at over 25,000 of both sexes – the women, however, being in the majority.

Guided

1 (a) P-E-E paragraphs are a good way to structure your answer to a comparison question. Finish this point about the ideas expressed in the extracts above:

Both texts start by expressing ideas about ....

....

(b) Now finish the P-E-E paragraph by making a comparison. Add evidence from each extract, and explain how the evidence supports your point above.

Hanson feels ....

....

whereas 'Occupations Accessible to Women' ....

....

Read the full extracts on pages 103 and 104.

2 Identify one more of each writer's ideas. For each one, find a short quotation as evidence.

Text 1: ....

....

Text 2: ....

....

3 Using your answer to Question 2, choose one idea from each extract. Write a P-E-E paragraph comparing the two texts.

....

....

....

....

Had a go ☐ Nearly there ☐ Nailed it! ☐

Comparing perspective

Read the short extracts 1 and 2 below. They are the opening paragraphs of two texts about parenting. Then answer Questions 1 and 2.

Extract 1: from 'The Rearing and Management of Children'

It is commonly believed that no harm can come of letting a child have its own way, so long as it is a mere babe. But this is a serious delusion.

Extract 2: from *The Boys Are Back in Town*

The fact is, I run a pretty loose ship. There's a lot of give in the structure. In our world of fuzzy logic and more-or-less, we need a lot of give to get by.

1 The opening sentence of Extract 1 from 'The Rearing and Management of Children' makes it clear that the writer feels that children need rules. How does Simon Carr's perspective on parenting compare with this view?

....

....

....

Guided **2** Complete this comparison explaining how each writer uses language to show their perspective.

In 'The Rearing and Management of Children', the writer uses the emotive phrase 'a serious delusion', which helps to show the writer's strong feelings about obedience. In *The Boys Are Back in Town* ....

....

....

....

Read the full extracts from 'The Rearing and Management of Children' on page 105 and *The Boys Are Back in Town* on page 100. Pay particular attention to the way they end. Then answer Question 3.

It is a good idea to look at differences between the beginning and ending of a text when you are thinking about perspective. This will also help you to compare the structure of texts.

3 Write a P-E-E paragraph comparing the writers' perspectives at the end of the extracts. Consider whether their perspectives have remained the same throughout or whether they end with a different point of view. Use one piece of evidence from each of the extracts.

....

....

....

....

....

Answering a compare question

When you compare the language used in two texts you can write about:

The main idea: what the texts are about

- Both texts are about ...
- On the other hand, **Extract 2** explores ...
- **Extract 1** is about ...

The perspective: the writers' point of view

- The writer of **Extract 1** feels ...
- **Extract 2** aims to ...
- The perspective of the writer is ...
- The perspective is shown through the writer's use of ...

negative | positive

The effect on the reader:

- Both texts aim to engage the reader but do so in different ways.
- **Extract 1** engages the reader by ...
- **Extract 2**, however, uses ...

create humour | influence | shock

Similar language features:

- Both texts use rhetorical questions, but use them to achieve different effects.
- **Extract 1** poses the question ...
- **Extract 2** uses a rhetorical question to ...

lists | pattern of three | figurative language | contrast | repetition | emotive language | hyperbole | sentence | structure

> Remember to make direct comparisons and that you can compare similarities and differences between the two texts.

1 Look again at the extracts from 'OK, you try teaching 13-year-olds' on page 103 and 'Occupations Accessible to Women' on page 104. Use the prompts above to write a paragraph comparing the different ways language and structure are used for effect in the two extracts. Remember to use quotations as evidence to support your points.

....

....

....

....

....

....

Had a go ☐ Nearly there ☐ Nailed it! ☐

Putting it into practice

1 Read the full extracts from 'The Rearing and Management of Children' on page 105 and *The Boys Are Back in Town* on page 100, then answer the exam-style question below.

Component 

To answer the following question you will need to use both texts.

A6. Both of these texts are about parenting and childhood. Compare:

- the writers' attitudes to parenting and childhood
- the ways in which they get across their ideas and arguments. **(10 marks)**

You must use the text to support your comments and make it clear which text you are referring to.

When you tackle this type of question in the exam, remember to:

- spend about 12 minutes on your answer
- read the question carefully and highlight the main focus
- spend a couple of minutes planning your answer before you start writing
- always write about both texts throughout your answer
- identify the language and structural devices used and comment on how they help the writer to get across their ideas and arguments.

Remember: You have more space than this to answer your question in the exam. Use your own paper to finish your answer to the question above.

Evaluating a text: fiction

Read the full extract from *Enduring Love* on page 99. Then read the exam-style question below. **You don't need to answer this question.** Instead, think about what it is asking you to do, then answer Question 1.

Component

Read from line 37 to the end.

A5. "In the final fifteen lines or so of this extract, the narrator is shown to be a natural leader." **(10 marks)**

To what extent do you agree with this view?

You should write about:

- your own impressions of the narrator as he is presented here and in the extract as a whole
- how the writer has created these impressions.

You must refer to the text to support your answer.

1 Read the following and circle what you should do when answering an evaluation question.

Focus closely on the specific lines given in the question, but also look at the whole text.	Use evidence from the text.	Focus closely on individual words and phrases, explaining connotations in detail.	Consider both sides of the argument when expressing your opinion.	Read the question carefully to make sure you evaluate the right aspect of the text.

Read part of a student's answer to Question A5 below. In the answer, the student is referring to this short section of the extract from *Enduring Love*:

> We were all talking at once. Two of us, myself and the motorist, wanted to walk the balloon away from the edge. Someone thought the priority was to get the boy out. Someone else was calling for the balloon to be pulled down so that we could anchor it firmly. I saw no contradiction, for we could be pulling the balloon down as we moved back into the field.

The narrator does not appear to be a natural leader at the start of this section as he ....

....

However, he then puts himself first when explaining an idea, for example ....

....

The writer uses repetition to ....

....

Guided **2** (a) Match the underlined sections of the student's answer to the underlined phrases in the short extract.

(b) Complete the student answer, adding evidence from the extract from *Enduring Love* and explanations to evaluate the extract.

When you evaluate, you need to comment on whether the impressions you get from the short extract are similar to or different from the impressions you get from the whole of the extract. Re-read the full extract from *Enduring Love* on page 99.

3 Does the whole extract suggest the narrator is a natural leader? Select one piece of evidence to back up your impression.

....

....

Use quotations to back up your points but you don't need to analyse the language or structure in detail.

Had a go ☐ Nearly there ☐ Nailed it! ☐

Evaluating a text: non-fiction

Read the exam-style question below. **You don't need to answer this question.** Instead, think about what it is asking you to do, then answer Question 1.

To answer the following question you will need to read the extract from 'Occupations Accessible to Women'.

A4. What do you think and feel about the view of female teachers presented in 'Occupations Accessible to Women'? **(10 marks)**

You should comment on:

- what is said
- how it is said.

You must refer to the text to support your comments.

1 Highlight or underline the key words in Question A4 above.

Now read this short extract from 'Occupations Accessible to Women', then answer Question 2.

> THE great difficulty of the educational question in the present day, and the obstacle to complete success in the earnest efforts made, is the difficulty, almost impossibility, of finding sufficiently-qualified teachers. The demand created by the Education Acts is estimated at over 25,000 of both sexes – the women, however, being in the majority.

2 Starting an answer with an overview that sums up your points shows you have a full understanding of the question. The overviews below were written in response to Question A4 using the extract above. Which one do you think is most effective? Circle your choice.

A The writer feels that there is a great problem with the education system.

B The writer's view is that there is a great shortage of female teachers.

C The writer's view is that it is extremely difficult to find suitably qualified female teachers.

Now read the short extract below. It is the final sentence from 'Occupations Accessible to Women'. Then answer Question 3.

> The comfort and advantage of possessing a small home would render the position of an elementary school-mistress <u>an eminently tempting one</u> to many a poor governess, <u>could she but manage to qualify</u> herself to hold the position.

Guided

3 What can you infer about the writer's view of female teachers from this final sentence? Has the viewpoint changed? Some phrases have been underlined to help you.

The ending of the article suggests that the writer feels ....

....

....

....

Using evidence to evaluate

Read this short extract from 'Occupations Accessible to Women', then answer Question 1.

> Some hard study would, in some cases, be needed to supply the inaccuracy of the general style of a woman's knowledge as a very thorough grounding in elementary subjects is needful. Very few, even the most highly-educated of women, can work a sum in fractions or proportion with rapidity, much less explain every step of the process so clearly as to bring it within the comprehension of a class; and how few who write good English from habit can teach the rules of grammar correctly.

Guided

1 Use the short quotations underlined in the extract above to explain the writer's perspective.

The writer feels that women are so poorly educated that only 'hard study' will overcome the 'inaccuracy' of their knowledge. The writer feels this situation is serious as he states ....

....

The writer emphasises this negative view of women's education by suggesting that they cannot work .... or .... This all suggests ....

....

Now read this short extract, taken from later in 'Occupations Accessible to Women', then answer Question 2.

> From various authorities we find the average income of the certificated mistresses of girls' schools to be reckoned at £58, and of infant schools at £56 per annum. They live, in addition, rent free, and in some cases allowances are made for fuel, light, etc. Under the School Boards of large towns higher emoluments are offered, £75 per annum having been fixed as the minimum salary for mistresses.

Guided

2 When evaluating, you can refer closely to the text by paraphrasing. Complete the following explanation by paraphrasing the information in the short extract above.

The writer feels that life for a female teacher can be very pleasant ....

....

....

When using quotations, remember that:
- short quotations are most effective
- you must use quotations rather than paraphrasing when explaining the effects of language
- all quotations must be in quotation marks and copied correctly from the text.

You can use longer quotations, but if you do you must be very careful about layout.

3 Which of the following should you **not** do when using a longer quotation? Circle your choice(s).

(a) Introduce it with a colon.

(b) Include it as part of your sentence.

(c) Start the quotation on a new line.

(d) Put the quotation in quotation marks.

Putting it into practice

1 Read the full extract from *One Day in the Life of Ivan Denisovich* on page 96, then answer the exam-style question below.

Component 1

Read from line 26 to the end.

A5. "In the final twenty or so lines of this extract, the writer encourages the reader to feel that Shukhov has found a way to deal with the hardship of the camp." **(10 marks)**

To what extent do you agree with this view?

You should write about:

- your own impressions of the way Shukhov handles life in the camp as he is presented here and in the extract as a whole
- how the writer has created these impressions.

You must refer to the text to support your answer.

When you tackle this type of question in the exam, remember to:

- spend around 12 minutes on your answer
- read the question carefully and highlight the main focus
- read the source text thoroughly, annotating as you read
- only use the lines of the text referred to in the question
- use inference and evidence from the text to explain your ideas and assess the effect of the text.

Remember: You have more space than this to answer your question in the exam. Use your own paper to finish your answer to the question above.

Putting it into practice

1 Read the full extract from 'The Rearing and Management of Children' on page 105, then answer the exam-style question below.

Component 

A4. What do you think and feel about the writer's view of bringing up children? **(10 marks)**

You should comment on:

- what is said
- how it is said.

You must refer to the text to support your comments.

When you tackle this type of question in the exam, remember to:

- spend around 12 minutes on your answer
- read the question carefully and highlight the main focus
- read the source text thoroughly, annotating as you read
- refer to the whole text unless specific lines numbers are given in the question
- use inference and evidence from the text to explain your ideas and assess the effect of the text.

Remember not to dismiss the ideas and views expressed in older texts as 'old-fashioned'.

Remember: You have more space than this to answer your question in the exam. Use your own paper to finish your answer to the question above.

Had a go ☐ Nearly there ☐ Nailed it! ☐

Writing questions: an overview

Both components of the English Language GCSE include a writing section: Section B.

1 Read the statements below. Decide which component each statement describes. Circle your choices.

(a) The focus is creative prose writing. **Component 1** **Component 2**

(b) The focus is transactional/persuasive writing. **Component 1** **Component 2**

(c) The writing section tests your ability to write for different purposes and audiences. **Component 1** **Component 2**

(d) The writing section tests your ability to write imaginatively and creatively. **Component 1** **Component 2**

(e) You will need to write one text from a choice of four titles. **Component 1** **Component 2**

(f) You will need to answer two questions. **Component 1** **Component 2**

Assessment objective 5

(a) Communicate clearly, effectively and imaginatively, selecting and adapting tone, style and register for different forms, purposes and audiences

(b) Organise information and ideas, using structural and grammatical features to support coherence and cohesion of texts

Assessment objective 6

Use a range of vocabulary and sentence structures for clarity, purpose and effect, with accurate spelling and punctuation

2 Now read these statements below about the assessment objectives tested in the writing sections. Decide which assessment objective each statement describes. Circle your choices.

(a) Tests whether you can communicate clearly, effectively and imaginatively. **AO5 AO6 Both**

(b) Tests how well you can use sentences and paragraphs to structure your writing effectively. **AO5 AO6 Both**

(c) Tests your vocabulary and whether you can use sentence structures for effect. **AO5 AO6 Both**

(d) Tests your spelling and punctuation. **AO5 AO6 Both**

(e) Tests how well you can organise information and ideas. **AO5 AO6 Both**

(f) Tests your ability to write in different forms, and for different purposes and audiences. **AO5 AO6 Both**

Guided

3 Summarise each assessment objective into one short sentence without using the words that are circled in the descriptions above.

Assessment objective 5 (a) Write ....

....

Assessment objective 5 (b) Arrange ....

....

Assessment objective 6 Use ....

....

Putting things into your own words and summarising ideas is a good revision technique. If you can summarise effectively, it shows that you fully understand what you are reading.

Writing questions: Component 1

Component 1 tests your creative prose writing skills.

1 Read the statements about Component 1 below.
Decide whether each statement is true or false.
Circle your choices.

(a) Your creative prose writing must take the form of a narrative or recount. **True False**

(b) You can write a poem. **True False**

(c) You can write a play. **True False**

(d) You should write between 450 and 600 words. **True False**

Turn to page 48 for a reminder about the assessment objectives.

2 (a) Which of the terms below is another word for 'narrative'? Circle your choices.

poem description story conversation

(b) Define the term 'recount'.

....

....

Look at the exam-style question below. **You don't need to answer this question**. Instead, consider the title choices the question gives, then answer Questions 3 and 4.

Component 1

Choose **one** of the following titles for your writing: **(40 marks)**

Either, (a) Making a Choice.

Or, (b) The Game.

Or, (c) Write about a time when you were at a theme park.

Or, (d) Write a story which begins:

I didn't think he would ever do it…

3 Which form should your writing take for title (a) in the exam-style question above? Circle your choice.

(a) narrative

(b) recount

(c) narrative or recount

4 Which form must your writing take for title (d) in the exam-style question above?

....

The table below shows three key stages of answering a Component 1 writing task.

Guided

5 Complete the table by writing the number of minutes you should spend on each stage. The first row has been done for you.

Total time for Component 1: Section B – Writing	45 minutes
Planning your answer	
Writing your answer	
Checking and proofreading your answer	

Writing questions: Component 2

Component 2 tests your skills in transactional or persuasive writing.

Guided

1 Cross out the incorrect words or phrases from the pairs below. Two examples have been done for you.

Transactional writing is usually:

- formal / ~~informal~~
- intended to achieve a specific purpose / amusing and light-hearted
- entertaining and humorous / serious, with humour only if appropriate to audience
- for a specific audience / suitable for all ages
- ~~open-ended~~ / carefully structured

Look at the exam-style questions below. **You don't need to answer these questions**. Instead, consider what they are asking you to do, then answer Question 2.

Turn to page 48 for a reminder about the assessment objectives.

Component 

B1. Your school/college is keen to encourage healthy eating.

Write a report for the Headteacher/Principal suggesting ways this might be done.

You could include:

- examples of what type of food is eaten at the moment
- your ideas about how healthy eating might be encouraged. **(20 marks)**

Component 

B2. A proposal has been made to set a curfew of 9pm in your local town, after which time all teenagers must return home.

You have decided to write an article for your local newspaper to share your views on this proposal. You could write in favour of or against this proposal.

Write an article for the newspaper giving your views. **(20 marks)**

2 (a) Circle the words in Question B1 that tell you which audience you should be writing for.

(b) Circle the words in each question that tell you the form the answer should take.

(c) Circle the words in each question that tell you, or suggest to you, what the purpose of your writing should be.

It is very important to organise your time in the exam carefully, to make sure you are able to answer both writing questions in Component 2.

3 You have a total of one hour for the Writing section in Component 2. Complete the table by writing in the number of minutes you should spend planning, writing and checking.

	Question B1	**Question B2**
Planning your answer		
Writing your answer		
Checking and proofreading your answer		

Writing for a purpose: creative

Look at the exam-style question below. **You don't need to answer this question now**. Instead, think about what you might include in a response to this title, then answer Questions 1 to 4.

Component 1

Write about a time when you were at a theme park. **(40 marks)**

Guided

1 Using the senses can help you to create a vivid picture in a reader's mind. Complete the table below to gather ideas you could use in your answer to the exam-style question above. Some ideas have been added for you.

At the theme park, I could...

see:	
hear:	
smell:	the sharp tang of diesel oil on the breeze
touch:	
taste:	syrupy sweet candy-floss

When you describe feelings, try to use verbs that show, rather than tell, the reader. This will make your writing more engaging.

Guided

2 The exam-style question above encourages you to write in the first person. This means you can describe the narrator's feelings in detail. Finish this sentence about how you were feeling at the theme park:

My face lit up with a wide smile and ....

....

....

Remember to keep the same narrative voice throughout your answer in the exam.

3 Figurative language will also help you to create strong descriptions and vivid images. For each of the following, write an imaginative example that you could use in a response to the exam-style question above.

Simile: ....

Metaphor: ....

Personification: ....

Using fewer well-chosen words is more effective than using too many unimaginative ones.

4 Write the first three sentences of your answer to the exam-style question at the top of this page. Use your answers to Questions 1 to 3 in your writing. Remember to choose your vocabulary carefully and try to use verbs that show rather than tell your feelings.

....

....

....

....

....

....

Had a go ☐ Nearly there ☐ Nailed it! ☐

Writing for a purpose: inform, explain, review

Look at the exam-style question below. **You don't need to answer this question now.** Instead, think about what you might include in a response to this title, then answer Questions 1 to 3.

Component 2

B1. Your local council is keen to encourage teenagers to use the local library.

Write a report for the council suggesting ways that this might be achieved.

You could include:

- examples of what is available in the library at the moment
- your ideas about how the council could improve library facilities. **(20 marks)**

Texts that inform, explain or review are all examples of transactional writing.

Guided

1 Transactional writing often uses headings and sub-headings to guide the reader and make the information easier to find. List up to four sub-headings that you could use to organise your answer to Question B1. An example has been done for you.

(a) Using social media to attract teenagers to the library

(b) ....

(c) ....

(d) ....

2 Using facts and statistics is an effective way to make your writing appear reliable. Write down four facts or statistics that you could include in your answer to Question B1.

(a) ....

(b) ....

(c) ....

(d) ....

3 Using the correct tone in your transactional writing is very important. Texts that inform, explain or review usually have a formal tone as they need to sound trustworthy. Write the opening paragraph of your answer to Question B1 above. Use a formal tone and try to use some of the facts and statistics from your answer to Question 2.

....

....

....

....

....

....

Remember that one of the questions in Component 2: Section B – Writing will be on the same topic as the reading texts in Section A. You may be able to use facts and statistics from one or both of these texts. You can make up facts and statistics too, as long as they are believable and appropriate.

In transactional writing, avoid using too much figurative language.

Writing for a purpose: argue and persuade

Look at the exam-style question below. **You don't need to answer this question**. Instead, think about what you might include in a response to this title, then answer Questions 1 to 4.

B2. A national newspaper has published an article suggesting that the internet is an addictive drug. You have decided to write a letter to the newspaper, sharing your views on this topic. You could write in favour of or against the suggestion in the newspaper article.

Write a formal letter to the newspaper giving your views. **(20 marks)**

1 Decide whether you want to write for or against the newspaper's suggestion in Question B2 above. Then write down three key points to support your point of view.

Point 1: ....

Point 2: ....

Point 3: ....

2 Write down a piece of evidence to support each of the points in your answer to Question 1.

Evidence for point 1: ....

Evidence for point 2: ....

Evidence for point 3: ....

Guided

3 A counter-argument allows you to dismiss an opposing point of view. Think about the points you made in Question 1 above. What opposing points might somebody on the other side of the argument make? How could you dismiss them? Write down your ideas.

Some people might feel ....

....

....

However, ...

....

Evidence could be facts or statistics, an expert opinion or an example from your personal experience. The evidence you use in your writing in the exam does not have to be real or true, but it must be believable.

4 Rhetorical devices can strengthen your argument. Choose one of the following devices and use it to re-write one sentence of your answer to Question 3.

rhetorical questions | direct address | repetition | lists | alliteration

contrast | pattern of three | emotive language | hyperbole

Had a go ☐ Nearly there ☐ Nailed it! ☐

Writing for an audience

Some Component 2 writing questions will clearly state the audience you should write for. Others will only hint at the audience. Look at the exam-style question below. **You don't need to answer it**. Instead, think about what you might include in a response to this title, then answer Questions 1 and 2.

Component 2

B2. A national newspaper has published an article stating that technology is ruining teenagers' lives. You have decided to write a letter to the newspaper giving your views on this topic. You could write in favour of or against the view given in the newspaper article.

Write a thoughtful article for the newspaper giving your views. **(20 marks)**

1 Describe the implied audience for this piece of writing. Include your thoughts on age and gender.

The audience is likely to be . . . .

. . . .

2 Which of the following sentences has the most appropriate tone and vocabulary for the audience you identified in Question 1? Circle your choice, then write a sentence to explain it.

A Some teenagers spend half their lives gawping at laptops and the telly, which I reckon is just such a waste of time.

B When you see a teenager staring at a computer, do not assume they are wasting their time.

Remember to think about how wide the implied audience might be. For example, although their main audience might be adults, newspapers are read by people of all ages.

. . . .

. . . .

Now look at this exam-style question. **You don't need to answer this question now**. Instead, think about the language you might use in your response, then answer Question 3.

Component 2

B1. Your school/college is keen to encourage students to lead a healthy lifestyle.

Write a speech for Year 11 students, encouraging them to take up a healthy lifestyle.

You could include:

- examples of the challenges of leading a healthy lifestyle
- your ideas about the benefits of a healthy lifestyle. **(20 marks)**

Guided

3 An answer to Question B1 has been started for you below. Add two sentences to this opening.

Let's get straight to the point. The whole 'eat your five-a-day' routine is boring. Especially when your parents hammer it home on a daily basis, and particularly when it's followed by the inevitable 'don't be a couch potato' speech. We don't always want to hear what's good for us. However, if what you really want is clear skin and to feel invigorated, then increasing the amount of green vegetables you eat is a good starting point.

. . . .

. . . .

. . . .

. . . .

Putting it into practice

Read the exam-style question below. **You don't need to answer this question**. Instead, think about the title options and what these might involve. Then answer Questions 1 and 2.

Component

Choose **one** of the following titles for your writing: **(40 marks)**

Either, (a) Growing up.

Or, (b) The Prom.

Or, (c) Write about your first day at school.

Or, (d) Write a story which begins:

I had no idea if I would be able to find it again...

When you tackle this kind of question in the exam, remember to:

- plan your time – you have 45 minutes for this question, including planning and checking
- read the question carefully and decide which title to answer
- plan your writing, including ideas about narrative voice and language techniques
- make sure the form you choose is a narrative (story) or a recount
- make sure you stick to the same narrative voice throughout your writing
- write 450 to 600 words.

1 (a) Choose one of the titles in the exam-style question above.

(b) Now plan the following for your chosen title:

Planning time: .... minutes

Writing time: .... minutes

Checking time:............... minutes

Form: ....

Narrative voice: ....

2 Note down some ideas about language techniques you could use in your answer. Write a sentence giving an example of each technique.

Technique 1: ....

Example 1: ....

....

Technique 2: ....

Example 2: ....

....

Technique 3: ....

Example 3: ....

....

Technique 4: ....

Example 4: ....

....

Had a go ☐ Nearly there ☐ Nailed it! ☐

Putting it into practice

Read the exam-style questions below. **You don't need to answer these questions**. Instead, think about what they are asking you to do, then complete the table.

Component 

B1. Your school/college is keen to encourage Year 11 students to be role models for younger students.

Write a report for the Headteacher/Principal suggesting ways this might be achieved.

You could include:

- examples of what might be involved in a role-model scheme
- your ideas about how students could be encouraged to take part. **(20 marks)**

Component 

B2. A proposal has been made to ban all dogs from your local park.

You have decided to write an article for your local newspaper to share your views on this proposal. You could write in favour of or against this proposal.

Write a lively article for the newspaper giving your views. **(20 marks)**

When you tackle these kinds of questions in the exam, remember to:

- plan your time – you have 1 hour to answer both questions, including planning and checking
- read the questions carefully and identify the topics
- annotate the question to highlight the form, audience and purpose
- plan your writing, including key features of the form and purpose
- spend an equal amount of time on each answer and write 300 to 400 words for each answer.

1 Plan responses to Questions B1 and B2 above by completing this table.

	B1	**B2**
Timing	Plan: minutes Write: minutes Check: minutes	Plan: minutes Write: minutes Check: minutes
Topic		
Form		
Audience		
Purpose		
Key features		

Form: articles and reviews

Read the exam-style question below. **You don't need to answer this question**. Instead, think about what it is asking you to do, then answer Questions 1 to 3.

B2. A proposal has been made to set a curfew of 9pm in your local town, after which time all teenagers must return home.

You have decided to write an article for your local newspaper to share your views on this proposal. You could write in favour of or against this proposal.

Write an article for the newspaper giving your views. **(20 marks)**

1 Think of a title you could use as a headline for the piece of writing in Question B2.

....

....

....

Headlines use a range of techniques including: repetition, a rhetorical question, alliteration, a pun or a rhyme.

2 Think of a sub-heading that will add more information to your headline.

....

....

3 Articles often use quotations from experts to make the information seem factual and reliable. Who could you quote in this article? What would they say?

....

....

....

Remember that the quotations or evidence you use in your writing in the exam do not have to be real or true, but they must be believable.

In the exam, you may be asked to write a review. Look at this exam-style question. **You don't need to answer this question now.** Instead, think about the language you might use in your response, then answer Question 4.

B1. Your school/college newspaper is launching a new reviews section and is asking for entries for the next edition.

Write an entertaining review of your favourite TV programme for the newspaper.

You could include:

- examples of what makes your chosen programme so watchable
- your ideas about why others should watch the programme. **(20 marks)**

Guided

4 Write an opening paragraph for the review in Question B1, using figurative language to engage the reader. If you wish, use the opening that has been started for you below. It is about the television programme *I'm A Celebrity... Get Me Out Of Here!*

In the jungle, the skies darken, the heavens open and a talentless celebrity nobody has ever heard of chokes on a handful of live maggots. My favourite television programme is like

....

....

....

Had a go ☐ Nearly there ☐ Nailed it! ☐

Form: letters and reports

Read this exam-style question. **You don't need to answer this question.** Instead, think about what you might need to include in your response, then answer Question 1.

B2. A national newspaper has published an article suggesting that school uniforms are a waste of money.

You have decided to write a letter to the newspaper to share your views on this suggestion. You could write in favour of or against this suggestion.

Write a letter to the newspaper giving your views. **(20 marks)**

1 Decide whether the following statements are true or false. Circle your choices.

(a) You should make it clear that you are writing a letter, for example by using 'Dear…'. **True** **False**

(b) You should use 'Dear Sir/Madam' if you don't know the name of the person you are writing to. **True** **False**

(c) You should use 'Yours sincerely' if you have used 'Dear Sir/Madam'. **True** **False**

(d) You should use a formal subject line to draw attention to your topic. **True** **False**

> If you are asked to write a letter in the exam, pay attention to the tone and content of your writing. You should also make it clear that you are writing a letter – for example, by using 'Dear…'.

Now read the following exam-style question. **You don't need to answer this question.** Instead, think about what might be needed for this piece of writing, then answer Questions 2 and 3.

B1. Your local council is keen to set up a youth parliament.

Write a report for the council suggesting ways this might be done.

You could include:

- examples of what a youth parliament could do
- your ideas about how to attract young people to join. **(20 marks)**

2 Reports need to be formal and factual. Write a headline and a suitable opening sentence for the report in Question B1 that give the main facts about the topic.

....

....

....

Guided

3 Reports are intended to inform their audience about a particular topic, and usually include recommendations. Look at the second bullet point in Question B1 above and suggest two recommendations you could use in your answer.

(a) Firstly, I would suggest ....

....

(b) ....

....

Form: information guides

Read this exam-style question. **You don't need to answer this question.** Instead, think about what you might need to include in your response, then answer Questions 1 to 4.

Component 

B1. Your local council is keen to encourage exchange visits between young people in your town or city and young people from other places in the UK.

Write an information guide for a teenage visitor to your town or city.

You could include:

- information about what there is to do and see
- practical advice to help the visiting teenagers find their way around. **(20 marks)**

1 Your information guide will need a heading or title to attract and engage the reader. Write down three possible headings for the guide in Question B1 using techniques such as alliteration, a pun or a pattern of three.

(a) ....

(b) ....

(c) ....

2 Choose the best of your headings in Question 1. Then explain why it would be the most effective for your teenage audience.

....

....

Guided

3 Sub-headings help to structure an information text and to guide the reader. Write down three sub-headings that you could use in your information guide for teenagers. An example has been done for you.

(a) Sensational sports ....

(b) ....

(c) ....

4 Lists are a useful way to get across a large amount of information. They are often used at the start of an information guide to signpost to the reader what will be included in the guide. What could you list at the start of your information guide for teenagers? Write a list using no more than four bullet points.

....

....

....

....

....

....

Lists can be bulleted, or numbered to show a sequence or ranking. Avoid using too many lists. You still need to show you can structure your writing to guide the reader, using sentences, paragraphs and adverbials. Go to page 71 to practise using adverbials.

Had a go ☐ Nearly there ☐ Nailed it! ☐

Putting it into practice

1 Answer the exam-style question below. Focus in particular on audience, purpose and format.

Component

B1. Your school is considering a new homework policy for all students.

Write a report for the Headteacher/Principal suggesting what should be included in the new policy.

You could include:

- examples of what happens at the moment
- your ideas about what the new policy should include. **(20 marks)**

When you tackle this type of question in the exam, remember to:

- read the question carefully and identify the topic, form, audience and purpose of the writing
- plan your writing before you start
- include all the relevant key features of the form and purpose
- spend 30 minutes on your answer, including planning and checking time
- write 300 to 400 words.

Remember: You have more space than this to answer your question in the exam. Use your own paper to finish your answer to the question above.

Ideas and planning: creative

Read this exam-style question. **You don't need to answer this question.** Instead, consider the creative prose title options, then answer Questions 1 to 3.

Component 1

Choose **one** of the following titles for your writing: **(40 marks)**

Either, (a) A Challenge.

Or, (b) The Trip of a Lifetime.

Or, (c) Write about a time when you were very scared.

Or, (d) Write a story which begins:

I don't remember clearly how it all began…

1 In the exam, you will need to choose a title quickly to save time for detailed planning. In the exam-style question above, circle the title you have the most initial ideas about.

2 Write down your initial ideas for the title you chose in Question 1, either as a list or a spider diagram.

Try to picture the scene or event in your mind. Think about the characters (e.g. who is there, what they are like) and the action (e.g. what is happening, what has happened already).

Guided

3 Now look at a student's plan for the title 'The Trip of a Lifetime', below. Add details to the plan, including ideas about creative writing techniques you could use.

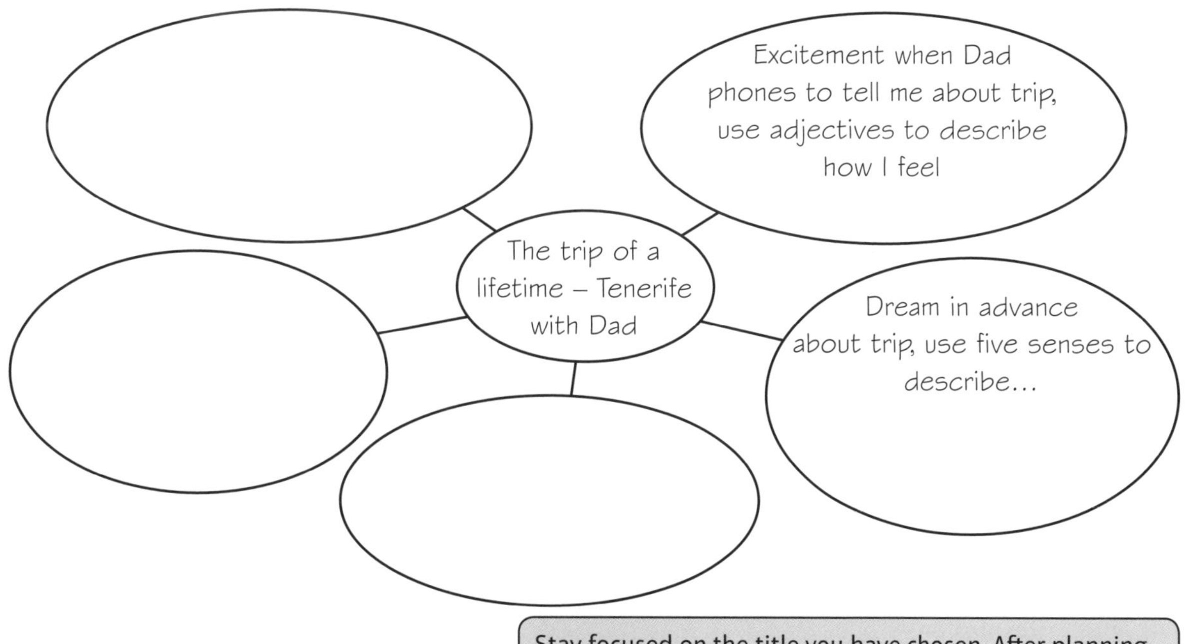

Stay focused on the title you have chosen. After planning, quickly check that all your ideas are centred on this title.

Structure: creative

It is important to structure your creative prose writing effectively. It is often best to use a narrative structure. Look at this exam-style question title. **You don't need to answer this question.** Instead, think about how you might structure an answer to this question, then answer Question 1 below.

Component 1

The Return. **(40 marks)**

Guided

1 Complete the narrative structure for this title below. Remember to include ideas about appropriate creative writing techniques in your plan.

Exposition: Relaxing in front of fire on windy winter day. Doorbell rings. I answer – it is my long-lost sister. Use dialogue.

Rising action: ....

....

Climax: ....

....

Falling action: ....

....

Resolution: ....

....

2 You can make a narrative more interesting, or tense, by playing with the narrative structure. Re-write your plan in Question 1, this time starting at the climax and using flashbacks to tell the story.

Climax:. ....

Exposition:. ....

Rising action: ....

Return to climax: ....

Falling action: ....

Resolution: ....

Beginnings and endings: creative

The beginning of your creative prose writing needs to engage the reader immediately and set the tone for the rest of the narrative or recount.

Look at this exam-style question title. **You don't need to answer this question now.** Instead, think about how you might begin and end an answer to this title, then answer Question 1 below.

Component 1

The Secret. **(40 marks)**

Guided

1 Write several different beginnings in response to this exam-style question title.

Don't be tempted to over-use dialogue. Mix it in with plenty of prose, to demonstrate your sentence structure skills.

Vivid description	**Dialogue** "I'm telling you, I saw her out there, clear as day!" hissed my aunt. "Ssh" whispered my father. "Just keep the secret until she's old enough to handle it!" Through the tiny crack in the door I could see my father's anguished face. My mind raced ahead imagining a million different scenarios, none of them happy. Could they really be talking about my long-lost mother?
Mystery	**Conflict or danger**

The ending of a piece of creative prose is just as important as the opening. Choose one of your openings from Question 1, then answer Questions 2 and 3.

2 What will the tone of your ending be? Will it be happy, tense or sad? Write a sentence explaining how you would end your story.

....

....

3 Write three possible final sentences. Make sure you focus on creating the tone you decided on in Question 2.

(a) ....

(b) ....

(c) ....

Make your ending as imaginative as possible. Avoid clichés like 'and they all lived happily ever after'.

Putting it into practice

Read the exam-style question below. **You don't need to answer this question.** Instead, think about the title options then answer Question 1.

Component 1

Choose **one** of the following titles for your writing: **(40 marks)**

Either, (a) Taking a Stand.

Or, (b) The Game.

Or, (c) Write about your favourite childhood memory.

Or, (d) Write a story which begins:

I didn't think he would ever do it…

When you plan for this type of question in the exam, remember to:

- read each title option carefully
- decide which title to answer
- spend 10 minutes on a detailed plan
- plan the narrative voice and creative writing techniques you will use.

1 Choose one of the title options from the exam-style question above. Then use the space below to plan your answer.

Ideas and planning: inform, explain, review

Read the exam-style question below. **You don't need to answer this question.** Instead, think about what it is asking you to do, then answer Question 1.

Component 2

B1. Your school/college is keen to help Year 7 students cope well with their first year at secondary school.

Write a report for the Head of Year 7 giving your ideas on how this could be achieved.

You could include:

- examples of what support already exists at your school
- your ideas about what additional support could be provided. **(20 marks)**

Use the bullet points in the question to support your planning.

Guided

1 Plan an answer to Question B1. Work through the planning stages below and then complete the spider diagram. Some ideas have been added for you.

(a) Plan your introduction. Tell your reader what you are writing about and why it is important.

(b) You will need three or four key points. Decide which key points you will include.

(c) Add detailed ideas to each of your key points, including techniques appropriate to your audience and purpose.

(d) Number your key points. Which will work best at the beginning and which at the end?

(e) Plan your conclusion.

(f) Add ideas for temporal adverbials that would help to guide your reader through your points.

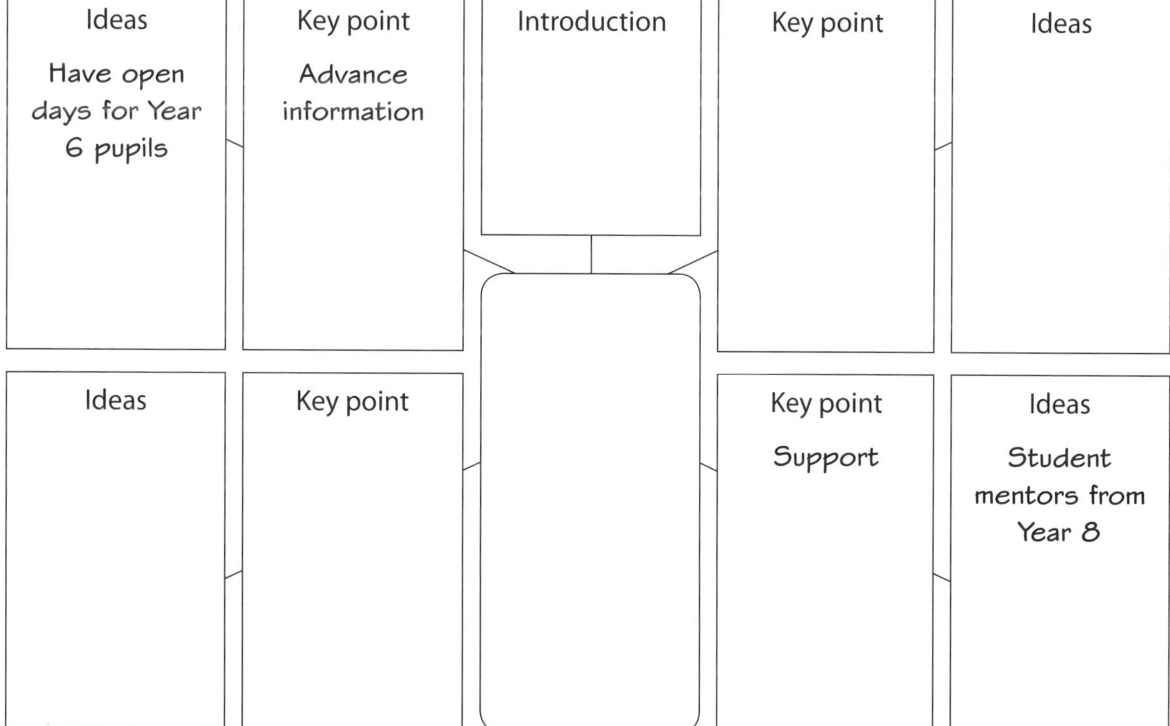

Remember that you must complete two writing tasks for Component 2. You only have 30 minutes for each task, including five minutes for planning. Plan your writing carefully – quality is more important than quantity.

Had a go ☐ Nearly there ☐ Nailed it! ☐

Ideas and planning: argue and persuade

Read the exam-style question below. **You don't need to answer this question.** Instead, think about what it is asking you to do, then answer Question 1.

B2. A proposal has been made to scrap exams on the grounds that they do not give a fair and accurate picture of a student's real abilities.

You have decided to write an article for your community magazine sharing your views on this proposal. You could write in favour of or against this proposal.

Write a thoughtful article for the magazine giving your views. **(20 marks)**

1 Plan an answer to Question B2. Work through the planning stages and complete the spider diagram below.

(a) Decide whether you agree or disagree with the point of view in the question. Summarise your response in the centre of the spider diagram below.
(b) To guide readers, plan an introduction that tells them what you are writing and why they should read it. Add it to the spider diagram.
(c) Decide on the **three** key points you will make.
(d) Decide on the evidence you will use to support your key points.
(e) Sequence your key points by numbering them. What would be the most logical or effective order?
(f) Add a counter-argument to your plan. What might someone who opposed your opinion argue? How can you dismiss their argument?
(g) Plan a conclusion that will reinforce your point of view.

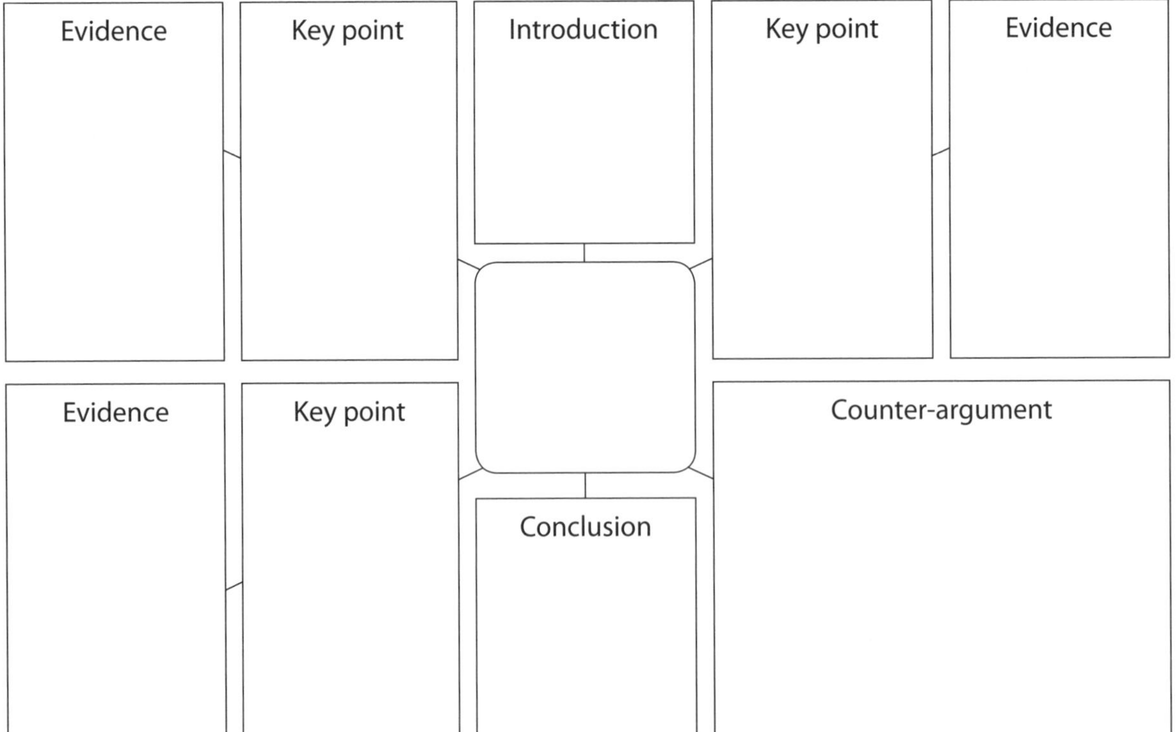

Remember:
- you only have **20 minutes** to plan, write and check this task – so aim for six paragraphs of well-crafted writing
- quality is rewarded – quantity is not.

Openings: transactional/ persuasive

Read the exam-style question below. **You don't need to answer this question now.** Instead, think about what it is asking you to do, then answer Questions 1 and 2.

B2. A national newspaper has published an article suggesting that sending people to prison does not prevent serious crime.

You have decided to write an article for the same newspaper to share your views on the subject. You could write in favour of or against the views given in the original article.

Write an article for the newspaper giving your views. **(20 marks)**

Guided

1 The first sentences of your writing must grab the reader's attention and make them want to read on. Try writing the opening sentence of your response to Question B2 in lots of different ways.

Using a rhetorical question: ....

....

Making a bold or controversial statement: ....

....

With a relevant quotation: ....

....

With a shocking or surprising fact or statistic: ....

....

With a short, relevant, **interesting** anecdote: My frail, elderly grandmother never recovered from a mugging. It happened in her own road, in broad daylight, in front of several dozen witnesses.

2 Choose one or two of your ideas from Question 1 and write the rest of your introduction to Question B2 above. Remember your introduction needs to introduce:

- the topic you are writing about
- your argument.

....

....

....

....

....

....

Don't tell the reader what you are going to be writing in your article:

In this article I am going to argue that ...

Just write it!

Had a go ☐ Nearly there ☐ Nailed it! ☐

Conclusions: transactional/ persuasive

Read the exam-style question below. **You don't need to answer this question now.** Instead, think about what it is asking you to do, then answer Questions 1 and 2.

Component 

B2. A national newspaper has published an article suggesting that sending people to prison does not prevent serious crime.

You have decided to write an article for the same newspaper to share your views on the subject. You could write in favour of or against the views given in the original article.

Write an article for the newspaper giving your views. **(20 marks)**

Guided

1 The final paragraph or conclusion of your writing should make a lasting impression. Try writing sentences you could include in your conclusion to Question B2, using the techniques below. An example has been done for you.

End on a vivid image: ....

....

End on a warning: ....

....

End on a happy note: ....

....

End on a thought-provoking question: How many vulnerable old people will be violently assaulted?

End on a 'call to action': ....

....

Refer back to your introduction, but don't repeat it: ....

....

2 Choose one or two of your ideas from Question 1 and write your conclusion to Question B2 above.

....

....

....

....

....

....

....

....

Look back over your whole argument. Consider how you might sum it up to end your piece of writing neatly and leave your reader with a clear message.

Putting it into practice

Read the exam-style question below. **You don't need to answer this question.** Instead, think about what you are being asked to do, then answer Question 1.

Component 2

B1. Your local community magazine has introduced a 'What's On' section and has invited readers to contribute.

Write a review for the magazine about an event you have attended in your local area.

You could write about:

- a film, concert or activity day
- what made the event particularly memorable and why other people might enjoy it. **(20 marks)**

When you plan for this type of question in the exam, remember to:

- read the question carefully and identify the topic
- identify the form, audience and purpose before you start
- spend 5 minutes planning your answer
- note down the features and techniques you will use to support the form, audience and purpose
- organise and sequence your ideas
- plan your introduction and conclusion.

1 Use the space below to plan your answer to Question B1 above.

Paragraphing for effect

Look at this exam-style question.

Component 2

B2. Your local newspaper has published an article suggesting that more careers advice should be offered in schools.

You have decided to write an article for the newspaper to share your views on this subject. You could write in favour of or against the views given in the original article.

Write an article for the newspaper giving your views. **(20 marks)**

Read this student's response to Question B2 then answer Questions 1 to 4.

> When students choose their GCSE options in Year Nine, they do not always choose subjects because they will help them in their future career. I chose my GCSEs either because I liked the teacher or because lots of my friends had chosen that subject. Neither of these reasons are sound. With more advice on the careers available to us and the different ways we can prepare for them, students would make more informed and more sensible decisions.

This student has organised the paragraphs in her argument using Point–Evidence–Explanation.

1 Identify and label the three different sections of this paragraph: point, evidence and explanation.

2 Plan your own Point–Evidence–Explanation paragraph in answer to Question B2 above.

Point: ....

Evidence: ....

Explanation: ....

3 Now write the paragraph you have planned in full.

....

....

....

....

....

....

....

....

....

4 Identify and label the three different sections of your paragraph: **point**, **evidence** and **explanation**.

Each time you start a new point, start a new paragraph. If you are writing to inform, explain or describe, start each paragraph with a topic sentence.

Linking ideas

Different adverbials have different purposes.

Guided

1 Copy the adverbials below into the table, adding each one to the correct column.

Consequently	Furthermore...	In particular	Significantly
For example	However	In the same way	Similarly
For instance	On the other hand	Moreover...	Therefore

Adding an idea	Explaining	Illustrating	Emphasising	Comparing	Contrasting
		For example			

Remember that time or temporal adverbials – such as afterwards, before, meanwhile – are very useful for indicating the passage of time in creative prose writing.

Read the exam-style question below. **You don't need to answer this question now.** Instead, think about what it is asking you to do, then answer Questions 2 and 3.

Component 2

B2. A proposal has been made to scrap exams on the grounds that they do not give a fair and accurate picture of a student's real abilities.

You have decided to write an article for your community magazine sharing your views on this proposal. You could write in favour of or against this proposal.

Write a thoughtful article for the magazine giving your views. (20 marks)

2 Look at the paragraphs below. They are extracts from one student's response to Question B2. Fill in all of the gaps using appropriate adverbials.

Many students are enormously successful in areas which exams do not or cannot assess. ...., one student at my school runs his own business designing websites for local companies. This is not something he has learned at school and .... his success will not be reflected in his exam results.

......................., some students' success depends not on hard work but on natural ability. .... this has more impact on less academic students. One student, ..., might achieve an A grade with little or no hard work, while another might have worked solidly and consistently for years to achieve a 'C'.

3 Now write your own Point–Evidence–Explanation paragraph in response to Question B2 above. Remember to use a range of adverbials to guide the reader through your argument.

Look back at your planning on page 66 to help you.

....

....

....

....

....

Putting it into practice

1 Answer the exam-style question below. Focus in particular on your use of paragraphs and adverbials.

Component 2

B1. Your school is planning to build a new canteen and is keen to involve students in the design process.

Write a report for the planning committee giving your views on the new canteen.

You could include:

- examples of what should be included in the canteen
- your ideas about how students could be involved in running the new canteen. **(20 marks)**

When you tackle any writing question in the exam, remember to:

- write in paragraphs
- plan one main point or idea per paragraph
- use P-E-E to structure your paragraphs
- organise and sequence your paragraphs
- use adverbials to link your paragraphs and guide your reader through your ideas.

Remember: You have more space than this to answer your question in the exam. Use your own paper to finish your answer to the question above.

Vocabulary for effect: synonyms

Synonyms are words with similar meanings. You can use them to avoid repetition and to add variety to your writing.

1 Look at the sentence below. Think of **at least two** synonyms for each circled word.

Synonyms for 'students':

1 ....

2 ....

3 ....

Synonyms for 'improve':

1 ....

2 ....

3 ....

Students can improve their learning by doing more revision.

Synonyms for 'learning':

1 ....

2 ....

3 ....

Synonyms for 'doing':

1 ....

2 ....

3 ....

If you get stuck, use a thesaurus – but first TRY to use the large vocabulary that you already have in your head. Remember, you won't have access to a thesaurus in the exam.

Guided

2 Look at each of the words in the table below. Complete the table by adding at least two synonyms for each word. An example has been done for you.

embarrassed	upset	scream	moment	annoyed
humiliated ashamed mortified				

Look at the exam-style question title below. Think about what you might include in a response to this title, then answer Question 3.

Component 1

Write about your most embarrassing moment. **(40 marks)**

3 Write a paragraph in response to the exam-style question above. Use some of your vocabulary from Question 2 in your writing.

....

....

....

....

....

Had a go ☐ Nearly there ☐ Nailed it! ☐

Vocabulary for effect: argue and persuade

Emotive words are important when you are writing to argue or persuade.

Guided

1 Look at the sentences below. Rewrite them, using emotive language to add more impact.

A Animals in laboratories are often treated really badly and then put to sleep.

Animals in laboratories are frequently treated cruelly and then slaughtered.

B If we continue to use too many of the earth's resources, the world will not have enough food.

....

....

C Our lives are filled with computers. We may not like it but we cannot do much about it.

....

....

2 Look at this sentence:

Some parents greeted the school's controversial plans with a (cry) of disapproval.

What would be the impact of replacing the circled word with either roar, howl or whimper?

(a) roar : ....

(b) howl : ....

(c) whimper : ....

Look at the exam-style question below. **You don't need to answer this question now.** Instead, think about what you might include in a response to this question, then answer Question 3.

Component ②

B2. An article in a community magazine claims that social networking is a waste of time.
You have decided to write an article for the magazine to share your views on this subject.
You could write in favour of or against the views given in the original article.
Write an article for the magazine giving your views. **(20 marks)**

3 Write two sentences in response to Question B2 above. Aim to choose vocabulary for its impact and its connotations.

....

....

Language for different effects 1

You can add power and impact to your writing by using a range of language techniques.

Guided

1 Look at the extracts from students' writing below. Some are taken from a piece of creative writing, some from a piece of transactional writing. Connect the rhetorical devices to the extracts.

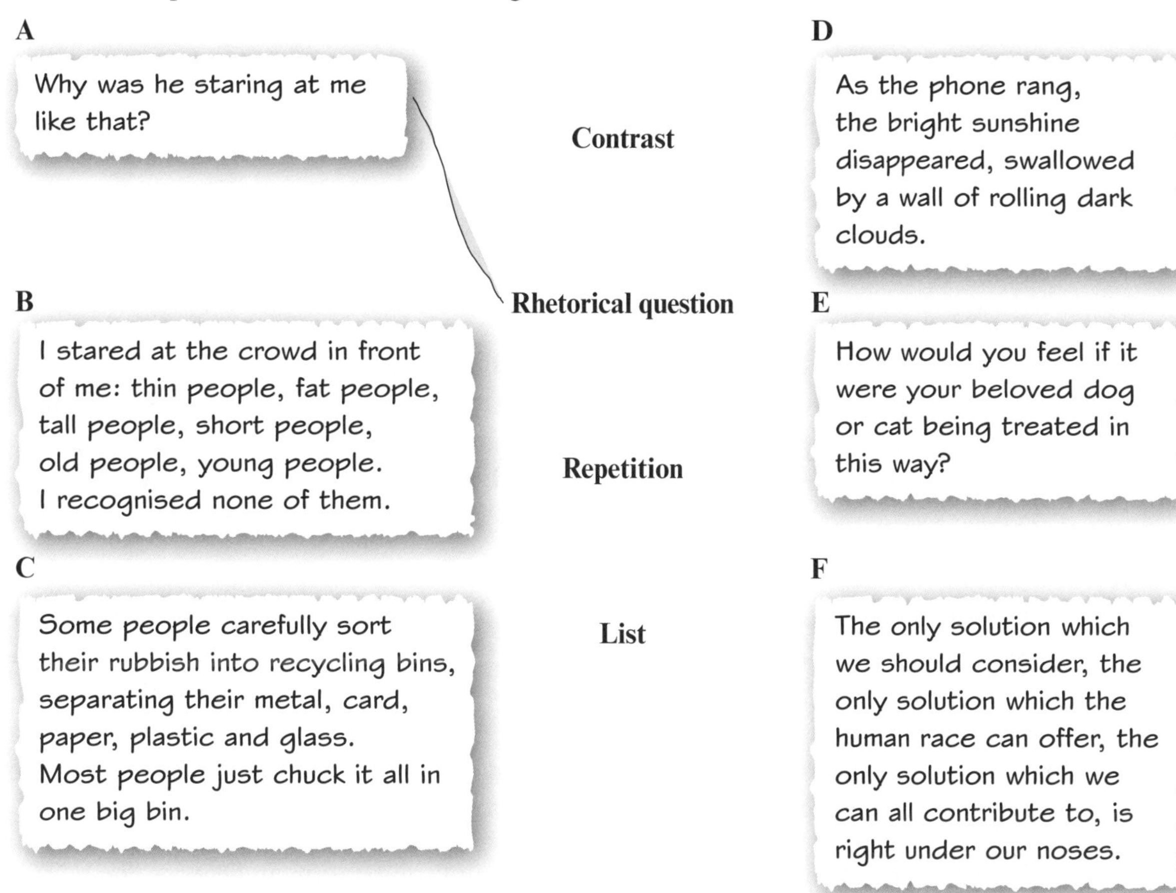

A
Why was he staring at me like that?
B
I stared at the crowd in front of me: thin people, fat people, tall people, short people, old people, young people. I recognised none of them.
C
Some people carefully sort their rubbish into recycling bins, separating their metal, card, paper, plastic and glass. Most people just chuck it all in one big bin.
Contrast
Rhetorical question
Repetition
List
D
As the phone rang, the bright sunshine disappeared, swallowed by a wall of rolling dark clouds.
E
How would you feel if it were your beloved dog or cat being treated in this way?
F
The only solution which we should consider, the only solution which the human race can offer, the only solution which we can all contribute to, is right under our noses.

Now look at the exam-style question below. **You don't need to answer this question now.** Instead, think about the language techniques you might use in a response, then answer Question 2.

B2. A proposal has been made to stop new drivers from taking their test until they are 21.

You have decided to write an article for your local newspaper to share your views on this proposal. You could write in favour of or against the proposal.

Write an article for the newspaper giving your views. **(20 marks)**

2 Write up to four short extracts from an answer to Question B2 above. Use one or more of the language techniques explored in Question 1 in each extract.

. . . .

. . . .

. . . .

. . . .

. . . .

. . . .

. . . .

. . . .

Had a go ☐ Nearly there ☐ Nailed it! ☐

Language for different effects 2

You can add power and impact to your writing by using a range of language techniques.

1 Look at the extracts from students' writing below. Some are taken from a piece of creative writing, some from a piece of transactional writing. Connect the rhetorical devices to the extracts in which they are used.

A

For about the hundredth time that day, my sister started sobbing.

B

How would you feel if it were your beloved dog or cat being treated in this way?

C

The city stretched before me, dark, dangerous and disturbing.

Direct address

Pattern of three

Alliteration

Hyperbole

D

This is an appalling waste of money. We might as well be setting light to wads of ten pound notes and laughing as we do it.

E

We must act intelligently, decisively and immediately.

F

Don't just sit there! Get off the sofa and do something.

Now look at the exam-style question below. **You don't need to answer this question now.** Instead, think about the language techniques you might use in a response, then answer Question 2.

Component 2

B1. Your local newspaper is holding a speech-writing competition and entries are invited under the heading 'School is cruel'.

Write an engaging speech as your competition entry.

You could include:

- examples of ways in which school might be considered 'cruel'
- your ideas about what changes could be made to make school more enjoyable. **(20 marks)**

2 Write up to four short extracts from an answer to Question B1 above. Use one or more of the language techniques explored in Question 1 in each extract.

. . . .

. . . .

. . . .

. . . .

. . . .

. . . .

. . . .

. . . .

. . . .

. . . .

Language for different effects 3

Figurative language can be used to create powerful images in the mind of a reader.

Guided

1 Look at the examples of figurative language used in the sentences below. The writers have used similes, metaphors and personification to give their writing impact. But which sentence uses which technique? Circle the correct answer.

A	The wind sang in the trees and the branches waved.	simile	metaphor	personification
B	The school has a challenging task ahead – an Everest to be climbed.	simile	metaphor	personification
C	She smiled like a tiger, licking its lips at the sight of a lost child.	simile	metaphor	personification
D	Waiting for the exams to begin is like waiting on death row.	(simile)	metaphor	personification
E	Homework is a ball and chain around every students' ankle.	simile	metaphor	personification
F	It's at that moment that your completely empty revision timetable creeps up behind you, taps you on the shoulder and asks if it could 'have a word'.	simile	metaphor	personification

Now look at the exam-style question below. **You don't need to answer this question now.** Instead, think about the figurative language you might use in a response, then answer Question 2.

Component 2

B2. Your school/college is proposing to change the school day so that it starts at 10.30am and continues into the early evening.

You have decided to write to the school/college governors giving your views on the proposed change. You could write in favour of or against this proposal.

Write a letter to the governors giving your views. **(20 marks)**

2 Write up to four short extracts from an answer to Question B2 above. Use one of the figurative devices explored in Question 1 in each extract.

. . . .

. . . .

. . . .

. . . .

. . . .

Had a go ☐ Nearly there ☐ Nailed it! ☐

Using the senses

Look at the examples of descriptive language used in the extracts below. The writer has used the five senses in an effort to engage the reader and make the descriptions more vivid.

A Strange aromas wafted in through the vents in the basement wall...

B Dusty wooden floorboards creaked in time to my footsteps...

C I could see the smoke wafting from the chimney of the empty house...

D Bitter juices filled my mouth as my hand brushed against...

E A large, red, crispy looking pizza was fresh from the oven. It lay in a pan on the hob, sizzling and dripping its aromatic juices.

1 Circle the two extracts that you feel are particularly effective.

2 Why are the two examples you have selected so effective? Write one sentence explaining how each example engages the reader.

Example 1 ....

....

Example 2 ....

....

Look at the exam-style question title below. **You don't need to answer this question now.** Instead, think about what you might include in a response to this title, then answer Question 3.

Component 1

The Haunted House. **(40 marks)**

3 Write the opening paragraph of a response to this exam-style question. Try to:

- use at least three of the five senses
- include examples of figurative language such as similes, metaphors and personification.

> Try to avoid starting sentences with phrases such as 'I could smell...' or 'I saw...'. Creative writing is far more effective if you 'show' rather than 'tell' the reader.

....

....

....

....

....

....

....

....

Narrative voice

Look at the creative prose extracts below, then answer Question 1.

A	In the end it didn't matter. I lost the game all on my own that day.	first person	third person	omniscient third person
B	She had expected somebody tall, dark and handsome. He had hoped for somebody short and cuddly. As she looked down, he reached up to shake her slender, bony hand. They both realised that if the date was to work, they would need to learn the art of compromise.	first person	third person	omniscient third person (circled)
C	To be honest it was all a huge fuss and about practically nothing. It wasn't as if I had actually killed anybody.	first person	third person	omniscient third person
D	Sheila seemed to have no conscience; she seemed to positively enjoy seeing other people in pain. Tears ran down Carol's face in great streaks but Sheila's only concern was the queue for a taxi. They were going to be very late unless the girl pulled herself together very quickly.	first person	third person	omniscient third person

Guided

1 For each extract above, identify the narrative voice. Circle the correct answers. An example has been done for you.

Look at the exam-style question title below. **You don't need to answer this question now.** Instead, think about how you might open a response to this title, then answer Question 2.

Component 1

Taking a Stand. **(40 marks)**

2 Write two possible openings of a response to this exam-style question. Aim to write one or two sentences for each opening. Use a different narrative voice in each opening.

Remember:
- Always check whether the question tells you which narrative voice to use.
- An omniscient third-person narrator can see into any character's mind.
- If you want to allow your reader to feel very close to your main character, use first-person narration.

(a) ....

....

(b) ....

....

Putting it into practice

1 Answer the exam-style question below. Focus in particular on your use of language and language techniques for effect.

Component 2

B2. The government is proposing to double the tax on takeaway food in an effort to encourage the population to adopt healthy eating habits.

You have decided to write a letter to your local MP to share your views on this proposal. You could write in favour of or against this proposal.

Write a thoughtful letter to your MP giving your views. **(20 marks)**

When you tackle any writing question in the exam, you should think about language. Remember to:

- annotate the question to highlight the format, audience and purpose
- choose language that is appropriate for the audience and purpose
- choose language techniques with care and for impact
- avoid using too many techniques – it is more important that your writing is well structured and appropriate for the audience and purpose.

Remember: You have more space than this to answer your question in the exam. Use your own paper to finish your answer to the question above.

Putting it into practice

1 Write a response to the exam-style question title below. Focus in particular on your use of language and language techniques for effect.

The Locked Room. **(40 marks)**

When you tackle any writing question in the exam, you should think about language. Remember to:

- choose language that is appropriate to your audience
- make ambitious and effective vocabulary choices to engage your reader
- use a range of language techniques
- avoid using too many examples of simile, metaphor or personification – a few original ideas are far more effective than a mass of clichés.

Remember: You have more space than this to answer your question in the exam. Use your own paper to finish your answer to the question above.

Had a go ☐ Nearly there ☐ Nailed it! ☐

Sentence variety 1

Using a range of different sentence types adds variety to your writing and helps to convey your ideas clearly and engage your reader.

Guided

1 Look at the sentences below and identify the sentence type. Are they:

A a single-clause sentence

B a multi-clause sentence with a subordinate clause

C a multi-clause sentence with a coordinate clause

D a multi-clause sentence with a relative clause

E a minor sentence?

For each one, identify the sentence type by writing a letter in the space. Then write a sentence to explain how you know. One has been done for you.

(a) We must act now because soon it may be too late.

Type: .... Explanation: ....

(b) Surely not.

Type: .... Explanation: ....

(c) I hurried but I was too late.

Type: .... Explanation: ....

(d) He gave her an apple.

Type: .... Explanation: It has only one clause, with just one verb.

(e) The bus, which should have been there at half past ten, failed to arrive.

Type: .... Explanation: ....

Look at the exam-style question below. **You don't need to answer this question now.** First, think how you might use different sentence types in a response.

Component 2

B2. A national newspaper has claimed that sportsmen and women are poor role models as they are liars, cheats and fakes.

You have decided to write an article for the newspaper to share your views about this claim. You could agree or disagree with the claim the newspaper has made.

Write a lively article for the newspaper giving your views. **(20 marks)**

Now consider this extract from one student's answer to Question B2, then answer Questions 2.

> Professional footballers are possibly the worst 'fakers'. With just one tap from another player they fall over. Sometimes they dive to the ground. Occasionally they fly. They always start screaming. It shows they are seriously injured. They say it was a foul. They demand a free kick. It is ridiculous.

2 The extract from the student's answer uses only short, single-clause sentences. Re-write the extract. Aim to use a variety of the four different sentence types.

....

....

....

....

....

Sentence variety 2

Look at the exam-style question title below. **You don't need to answer this question now.** Instead, think about what you might include in a response, then answer Questions 1 and 2.

Component 1

The Big City. **(40 marks)**

1 Write a sentence that you could use in your answer to the above exam-style question, beginning with the following. An example has been done for you.

(a) a pronoun (e.g. I, he, she, they): I grew up in a tiny village in the middle of nowhere.

(b) an article (e.g. a, an, the): ....

(c) a preposition (e.g. above, behind, between): ....

(d) an -ing word (or present participle) (e.g. running, hurrying, crawling): ....

(e) an adjective (e.g. slow, quiet, violent): ....

(f) an adverb (e.g. alarmingly, painfully, happily): ....

(g) a conjunction (subordinate clause + main clause) (e.g. if, although, because): ....

> Think about the first word of your sentences. Varying the first word adds interest to your writing.

2 Now write a paragraph in response to the above exam-style question. Aim to use:

- all seven different types of sentence opener in your writing
- a different word to start each of your sentences.

....

Had a go ☐ Nearly there ☐ Nailed it! ☐

Sentences for different effects

The ladder tipped over, the paint pot went flying, the paint exploded over her sofa, the paint pot hit her treasured vase, and the vase smashed into dust. I froze.

1 In the example above, a long sentence is followed by a short sentence. What effect is this intended to have on the reader?

....

....

Guided 2 In the sentences below the same ideas have been used, but in a different order.

A Before I walked the six miles home, I scrubbed every last drop of paint from the carpet and swept up every last crumb of glass, while she watched with a grim smile of quiet satisfaction on her lips.

B While she watched with a grim smile of quiet satisfaction on her lips, I scrubbed every last drop of paint from the carpet and swept up every last crumb of glass before I walked the six miles home.

How does the order in which the information is organised affect each sentence's emphasis?

The first sentence emphasises ....

....

....

....

Look at the exam-style question below. **You don't need to answer this question now.** Instead, think about how you might begin an answer, then answer Question 3.

Component 2

B1. Your school/college is keen to get students involved in raising funds for Children in Need.

Write a speech for a Year 11 assembly, encouraging students to get involved.

You could include:

- examples of sponsored activities students might take part in
- your ideas about why charity fundraising is important. **(20 marks)**

Avoid overloading a sentence with too much information spread over a number of subordinate clauses. This can cause the reader to lose attention.

3 Write the opening two or three sentences of your own response to Question B1 above. Aim to include a:

- long sentence followed by a short sentence
- sentence structured to give specific emphasis.

....

....

....

Putting it into practice

1 Answer the exam-style question below. Focus in particular on varying your sentences for effect.

2

B2. A national newspaper is running a campaign asking the Government to ban all students from bringing sugary drinks and snacks into school.

You have decided to write to the newspaper to share your views on this campaign. You could write in favour of or against this campaign.

Write a letter to the newspaper giving your views. (20 marks)

When you tackle any writing question in the exam, you should think about sentence variety. Remember to:

- use a range of sentence types
- start your sentences in a range of different ways
- structure your sentences for effect
- avoid overloading individual sentences with too much information.

Remember: You have more space than this to answer your question in the exam. Use your own paper to finish your answer to the question above.

Ending a sentence

Failing to use full stops, question marks, exclamation marks and capital letters correctly affects the quality of your writing.

1 When should you use a full stop? ....

2 When should you use a question mark? ....

Guided **3** What three mistakes should you avoid when using exclamation marks? An example has been done for you.

(a) You should avoid scattering exclamation marks randomly throughout your writing, and instead use them sparingly.

(b) ....

....

(c) ....

....

4 Look at the sentences below. Tick the two sentences that are punctuated correctly. Cross the one that is not.

A I knew that what she had done was wrong, I had to persuade her to do something about it.

B I knew that what she had done was wrong. I had to persuade her to do something about it.

C I knew that what she had done was wrong and I had to persuade her to do something about it.

> You do not use a comma to join two pieces of information in a sentence. Use a full stop to separate them or a conjunction to join them. So check every time you use a comma: should it be a comma or is the sentence complete?

Now write a sentence explaining your decision. ....

....

....

5 Look at this student's writing. Correct all the full stop, question mark and exclamation mark errors you can find.

A Change of Heart!!

I braced myself for a confrontation, she was looking at me like she knew I had something to say and she didn't want to hear it. My heart began to race and a strange throbbing pain pulsed in my forehead. How could I say it. How could I tell her what I was thinking without upsetting her.

She knew something was coming, tears were welling up in her dark brown eyes and her bottom lip was starting to quiver. I didn't feel much better than she did, my stomach was churning and I could feel my legs shaking. I tried to speak, my mouth felt like sandpaper, it was dry and rough and I couldn't form the words.

Commas

If you are confident with using commas, you will write more effective multi-clause sentences and lists.

Guided

1 Look at the sentences below. Some have used commas correctly. Some have not. Tick the correct sentences and cross the incorrect ones.

Commas in lists

- ✗ **A** They can comfort, us in a crisis help out when we're in trouble make us laugh or make us cry.
- ☐ **B** It doesn't matter whether they're tall, short, thin, fat, heart-stoppingly attractive or mirror-crackingly ugly.
- ☐ **C** She was loud, angry, obnoxious and painfully honest.

Commas in multi-clause sentences with subordinate clauses

- ✓ **D** Whether we like it or not, friends can hurt as well as help us.
- ☐ **E** Friends can hurt as well as help us whether we like it or not.
- ☐ **F** Although I had known her since primary school we never spoke again.

Commas in multi-clause sentences with relative clauses

- ☐ **G** The problem which we may not want to face, is that friends can sometimes let us down.
- ☐ **H** A friend who I will not name once told me all my worst faults.
- ☐ **I** Her house, which I only ever visited once, was enormous.

2 Look again at all the sentences in Question 1. Correct any that you marked as incorrect.

Look at the exam-style question title below. **You don't need to answer this question now.** Instead, think about what you might include in a response, then answer Question 3.

Component 1

The Perfect Friend. **(40 marks)**

Remember to end your sentences correctly. Avoid using a comma splice.

3 Write three to five sentences in response to the exam-style question above. Use commas correctly to separate:
- items in a list
- a main and subordinate clause
- a main and relative clause.

....

....

....

....

....

....

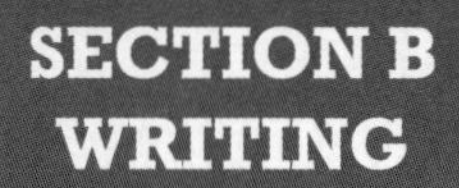

Had a go ☐ Nearly there ☐ Nailed it! ☐

Apostrophes and speech punctuation

Make sure you know how to avoid the common errors of missing out or using incorrect apostrophes and speech punctuation.

1 Look at the sentences below. Some have used apostrophes correctly. Some have not. Tick the correct sentences and cross the incorrect ones.

Apostrophes in contractions

☐ **A** I do'nt see her very often.

☐ **B** I can't believe how things turned out.

☐ **C** She wouldnt answer the phone.

Apostrophes of possession

☐ **D** My teachers' face was a picture.

☐ **E** The school's reaction was incredible.

☐ **F** The boys' faces all lit up.

Speech punctuation

☐ **G** 'I don't believe it!' she shouted.

☐ **H** 'Never mind.'

☐ **I** 'Come over here.' he whispered.

2 Look again at all the sentences in Question 1. Correct any that you marked as incorrect.

Guided 3 Now write a conversation between two friends in which they discuss a boy whose behaviour has resulted in several teachers ringing his parents. Aim to use apostrophes and speech marks correctly.

'Hey,' she called. 'Come over here.'

'What do you want?' I asked. ....

....

....

....

....

....

....

....

....

Remember:

- apostrophes in contractions are used to replace **missing letters**
- apostrophes of possession are always placed **at the end of the noun** whether it's plural (teachers') or singular (teacher's)
- in dialogue, there is always a punctuation mark **before** the closing speech marks.

Colons, semi-colons, dashes, brackets and ellipses

Punctuation helps you to express yourself clearly. It can also help you to develop your ideas.

1 Look at the sentences below. How could you alter or add to the punctuation, using a colon or a semi-colon?

Colons and semi-colons

A There is only one thing you can do to improve your grades. Revise.

B Teachers can help. They can give revision tips and answer any questions you have about the exam.

C Revision isn't easy. It takes time and willpower.

D Exams are the problem. Revision is the solution.

> You can use a semi-colon to link two connected ideas instead of using a conjunction. You can use a colon to introduce:
> - a list
> - an example
> - an explanation.

Dashes and brackets

Guided

2 Look at the sentences below. Some have used dashes and brackets correctly. Some have not. Tick the correct sentences and cross the incorrect ones. An example has been done for you.

☐ A My revision – which mainly involves staring into space – began this morning.

☐ B A short break (or sometimes a long break) helps clear your mind and recharge your battery.

☐ C My bedroom walls are covered in scribbled revision notes and key points (not a pretty sight.

☑ D Sometimes I wonder why I bother – and then I remember.

3 Look again at all the sentences in Question 2. Correct any that you marked as incorrect.

Look at the exam-style question title below. **You don't need to answer this question now.** Instead, think about what you might include in a response, then answer Question 4.

Component 1

Write about a time when you overcame a personal challenge. **(40 marks)**

4 Write three to five sentences in response to the exam-style question above. Try to use:
- a colon and a semi-colon
- dashes, brackets and an ellipsis.

. . . .

. . . .

. . . .

. . . .

. . . .

. . . .

. . . .

. . . .

. . . .

Putting it into practice

1 Answer the exam-style question below. Focus in particular on punctuation.

Component 2

B1. Your Headteacher/Principal wants to encourage students to take a more active role in the running of the school/college and has advertised for part-time student receptionists.

Write a letter applying for the job.

You could include:

- examples of what makes you the ideal candidate
- your ideas about what you could gain from the role.

(20 marks)

When you tackle any writing question in the exam, you should think about punctuation. Remember to:

- use a range of punctuation accurately, including advanced punctuation such as colons and semi-colons
- plan your time carefully so that you have time to check the accuracy of your punctuation.

Remember: You have more space than this to answer your question in the exam. Use your own paper to finish your answer to the question above.

Common spelling errors 1

Some of the most common spelling errors in students' writing are a result of misusing or confusing the following:

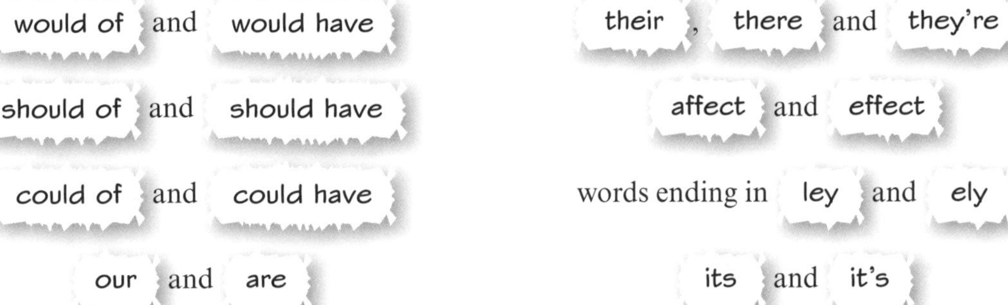

would of and would have
should of and should have
could of and could have
our and are
their, there and they're
affect and effect
words ending in ley and ely
its and it's

1 Identify and correct any spelling errors in these sentences.

A They went all the way back to there house.

B It would of been absolutley unbelievable – if I hadn't seen it with my own eyes.

C One affect of this issue is extremley concerning.

D Their first problem was how to get the students interested.

E Their our three reasons for this.

F There refusing to do anything about it.

G The school offered it's help immediately.

H We felt that students should definitley of been involved.

I Its not only the teachers who our effected by this situation.

J We were forced to reconsider are plan.

K It could not of been achieved without there help.

L Many students felt it had affected them negativley.

M Its not the first time this has happened.

- There are very few words ending in **ley**.
- **Would of**, **could of** and **should of** are **always** incorrect.

Had a go ☐ Nearly there ☐ Nailed it! ☐

Common spelling errors 2

Some of the most common spelling errors in students' writing are a result of misusing or confusing the following:

your and you're

of and off

two, too and to

whose and who's

we're, were, where and wear

passed and past

1 Identify and correct any spelling errors in these sentences:

A He did not know were he was going or who's idea it was.

B To many people make the same mistake.

C The time for worrying has past.

D This has taken some of the pressure of us.

E Your never sure whether you're doing enough to help.

F Whose going to complain about that?

G We where the first people there but still they ignored us.

H They walked passed us as though we wear invisible.

I They went too far, taking it too an extreme.

J How can we tell who's to blame?

K It can be difficult to know when your in the wrong.

L Support for the idea soon began to fall of.

M We simply don't know whose argument to believe and whether were expected to agree or not.

Remember:
A lot is two words. '**Alot** of people make this mistake' is wrong, but '**A lot** of people make this mistake' is correct.

Common spelling errors 3

Some of the most frequently misspelt words are explored in the table below. Make sure you learn how to spell these words properly.

argument	arguement	argumant
dificult	difficult	diffacult
disappoint	dissappoint	disapoint
disappear	dissappear	disapear
embarrassing	embarassing	embarasing
possesion	possession	posession
beggining	begining	beginning
recomend	recommend	reccomend
occassionaly	ocasionally	occasionally
definately	definitely	definitley
separately	seperately	seperatley
conscious	conshus	concsous
conshence	conscience	concsience
experiance	experance	experience
indapendance	independence	independance
beleive	believe	beleve
weird	wierd	weerd
business	busness	buisness
rythm	rhytm	rhythm
decision	desicion	desision
greatfull	grateful	greatful

1 Look carefully at the words in the table. In each row, one spelling is correct and two are incorrect. Tick the correct spelling and cross out the incorrect spellings.

> Correct spelling **can be learned**. Every time you spell a word incorrectly, make a note of the word and start to practise the correct spelling on a regular basis. Try strategies like looking for a hidden word within the word you are learning to spell, or saying what you see.

2 Now check your answers on page 127. Use the space below to write any spellings from the table above that you are unsure of. Practise them on a regular basis.

Had a go ☐ Nearly there ☐ Nailed it! ☐

Proofreading

Proofreading is important. In the exam, plan your time carefully so you have time to check your work for errors.

1 Look at the extract from one student's writing below. Read it carefully, looking for any:

- spelling errors
- punctuation errors
- grammatical errors – e.g. misused, repeated or missing words.

Circle and correct all the errors you can find.

> Scotland is the most amazing place Ive ever visited, even though it took ten hours to drive there it was worth it the moment i saw were we were staying. Huge blue lochs, rolling green hills, miles and miles of pine forest. They even looked beautiful driving passed them in a a car.
>
> On the first day we took the dogs for a long walk through a forest, it was the quitest place Ive ever been. Even with my brother their, all you could hear was the sound of leafs rustling in the breeze, the birds singing and you're heart beating.
>
> Are hotel was great, the scottish people are so frendly. I would definitley stay there again.

2 Look back at three or four pieces of writing you have completed recently. How many errors can you find? In the table below, note down words which you have misspelled and the **kinds** of punctuation and grammatical errors you have made.

Spelling errors	Punctuation errors	Grammatical errors

Train your proofreading brain to look out for the kinds of punctuation and grammatical errors you are prone to making. When the alarm rings, **stop!** Double check and correct any mistakes.

3 Use the space below to practise and learn all the spellings you have noted in the table.

Putting it into practice

1 Answer the exam-style question below. Focus in particular on proofreading your answer.

Component 

B1. Your school/college is keen to find out more about the pressures faced by young people.

Write a report for the Headteacher/Principal about the pressures teenagers like yourself face.

You could include:

- examples of the different kinds of pressure young people are under
- your ideas about how the school/college could help to reduce some of these pressures.

(20 marks)

When you tackle any writing question in the exam, remember to:

- save time after you have finished writing to check the accuracy of your writing
- look out for the spelling, punctuation and grammatical errors that you know you tend to make.

Remember: You have more space than this to answer your question in the exam. Use your own paper to finish your answer to the question above.

The novel from which this extract is taken follows a prisoner through one day of his long imprisonment in a Russian labour camp. The action takes place in 1951.

One Day in the Life of Ivan Denisovich

As usual, at five o'clock that morning reveille was sounded by the blows of a hammer on a length of rail hanging up near the staff quarters. The intermittent sounds barely penetrated the window-panes on which the frost lay two fingers thick and then ended almost as soon as they'd begun. It was cold outside, and the camp-guard was reluctant to go on beating out the reveille for long.

The clanging ceased, but everything outside still looked like the middle of the night when Ivan Denisovich Shukhov got up to go to the bucket. It was pitch dark except for the yellow light cast on the window by three lamps – two in the outer zone, one inside the camp itself.

And no one came to unbolt the barrack-hut door; there was no sound of the barrack-orderlies pushing a pole into place to lift the barrel of nightsoil and carry it out.

Shukhov never overslept reveille. He always got up at once, for the next ninety minutes, until they assembled for work, belonged to him, not to the authorities, and any old-timer could always earn a bit – by sewing a pair of over-mittens for someone out of old sleeve lining; or bringing some rich lag in the team his dry valenki – right up to his bunk, so that he wouldn't have to stumble barefoot round the heap of boots looking for his own pair; or going the rounds of the store-huts, offering to be of service, sweeping up this or fetching that; or going to the mess-hall to collect bowls from the tables and bring them stacked to the dishwashers – you're sure to be given something to eat there, though there were plenty of others at that game, more than plenty – and, what's worse, if you found a bowl with something left in it you could hardly resist licking it out. But Shukhov had never forgotten the words of his first team-leader, Kuziomin – a hard-bitten prisoner who had already been in for twelve years by 1943 – who told the newcomers, just in from the front, as they sat beside a fire in a desolate cutting in the forest:

"Here, lads, we live by the law of the taiga. But even here people manage to live. D'you know who are the ones the samps finish off? Those who lick other men's left-overs, those who set store by the doctors, and those who peach on their mates."

As for peachers, he was wrong there. Those people were sure to get through camp all right. Only, they were saving their own skin at the expense of other people's blood.

Shukhov always arose at reveille. But this day he didn't. He had felt queer the evening before, feverish, with pains all over his body. He hadn't been able to get warm all through the night. Even in his sleep he had felt at one moment that he was getting seriously ill, at another that he was getting better. He had longed for the morning not to come.

But the morning came as usual.

Anyway, it wasn't surprising that he'd felt cold in the night. That ice on the window-panes! And the white cob-webs of hoar-frost all along the huge hut where the walls joined the ceiling!

He didn't get up. He lay there in his bunk on the top tier, his head buried in a blanket and a coat, his two feet stuffed into one sleeve, with the end tucked under, of his wadded jacket. He couldn't see, but his ears told him everything going on in the barrack-room and especially in the corner his team occupied. He heard the heavy tread of the orderlies carrying one of the big barrels of nightsoil along the passage outside. A light job, that was considered, a job for the infirm, but just you try and carry out the muck without spilling any. He heard some of the 75th slamming bunches of boots on to the floor from the drying-shed. Now their own lads were doing it (it was their own team's turn, too, to dry valenki). Tiurin, the team-leader, and his deputy Pavlo put on their valenki, without a word but he heard their bunks creaking. Now Pavlo would be going off to the bread-stores and Tiurin to the staff quarters to see the P.P.D.

Ah, but not simply to report as usual to the authorities who distributed the daily assignments. Shukhov remembered that this morning his fate hung in the balance: they wanted to shift the 104th from the building-shops to a new site, the 'Socialist Way of Life' settlement. It lay in open country covered with snow-drifts, and before anything else could be done there they would have to dig pits and put up posts and attach barbed wire to them. Wire themselves in, so that they wouldn't run away. Only then would they start building.

There wouldn't be a warm corner for a whole month. Not a dog-kennel. And fires were out of the question. Where was the firewood to come from? Warm up with the work, that was your only salvation.

No wonder the team-leader looked so worried, that was his responsibility – to elbow some other team, some bunch of clod-hoppers, into the assignment instead of the 104th. Of course he wouldn't get the authorities to agree if he turned up empty-handed. He'd have to take a pound of pork-fat to the senior official there, if not a couple of pounds.

There's never any harm in trying, so why not have a go at the sick-bay and get a few days off if you can? After all, he did feel as though every limb was out of joint.

Aleksandr Solzhenitsyn

hoar frost, a type of frost
orderlies, people responsible for tasks like cleaning
peach, to tell on someone
P.P.D., Production Planning Department
reveille, a military term for a signal to wake up
valenki, knee-length boots for winter wear

The novel from which this extract is taken is set in Alabama in the United States in the 1930s. Key themes of the novel include racism, and how good and evil can coexist.

To Kill a Mockingbird

The following Monday afternoon Jem and I climbed the steep front steps to Mrs Dubose's house and padded down the open hallway. Jem, armed with Ivanhoe and full of superior knowledge, knocked at the second door on the left.

'Mrs Dubose?' he called.

Jessie opened the wood door and unlatched the screen door.

'Is that you, Jem Finch?' she said. 'You got your sister with you. I don't know – '

'Let 'em both in, Jessie,' said Mrs Dubose. Jessie admitted us and went off to the kitchen.

An oppressive odour met us when we crossed the threshold, an odour I had met many times in rain-rotted grey houses where there are coal-oil lamps, water dippers, and unbleached domestic sheets. It always made me afraid, expectant, watchful.

In the corner of the room was a brass bed, and in the bed was Mrs Dubose. I wondered if Jem's activities had put her there, and for a moment I felt sorry for her. She was lying under a pile of quilts and looked almost friendly.

There was a marble-topped washstand by her bed; on it were a glass with a teaspoon in it, a red ear syringe, a box of absorbent cotton, and a steel alarm clock standing on three tiny legs.

'So you brought that dirty little sister of yours, did you?' was her greeting.

Jem said quietly, 'My sister ain't dirty and I ain't scared of you,' although I noticed his knees shaking.

I was expecting a tirade, but all she said was, 'You may commence reading, Jeremy.'

Jem sat down in a cane-bottom chair and opened Ivanhoe. I pulled up another one and sat beside him.

'Come closer,' said Mrs Dubose. 'Come to the side of the bed.'

We moved our chairs forward. This was the nearest I had ever been to her, and the thing I wanted most to do was move my chair back again.

She was horrible. Her face was the colour of a dirty pillowcase, and the corners of her mouth glistened with wet, which inched like a glacier down the deep grooves enclosing her chin. Old-age liver spots dotted her cheeks, and her pale eyes had black pinpoint pupils. Her hands were knobby, and the cuticles were grown up over her fingernails. Her bottom plate was not in, and her upper lip protruded; from time to time she would draw her nether lip to her upper plate and carry her chin with it. This made the wet move faster.

I didn't look any more than I had to. Jem re-opened Ivanhoe and began reading. I tried to keep up with him, but he read too fast. When Jem came to a word he didn't know, he skipped it, but Mrs Dubose would catch him and make him spell it out. Jem read for perhaps twenty minutes, during which time I looked at the soot-stained mantelpiece, out of the window, anywhere to keep from looking at her. As he read along, I noticed that Mrs Dubose's corrections grew fewer and farther between, that Jem had even left one sentence dangling in mid-air. She was not listening.

I looked towards the bed.

Something had happened to her. She lay on her back, with the quilts up to her chin. Only her head and shoulders were visible. Her head moved slowly from side to side. From time to time she would open her mouth wide, and I could see her tongue undulate faintly. Cords of saliva would collect on her lips; she would draw them in, then open her mouth again. Her mouth seemed to have a private existence of its own. It worked separate and apart from the rest of her, out and in, like a clam hole at low tide. Occasionally it would say, 'Pt,' like some viscous substance coming to a boil.

I pulled Jem's sleeve.

He looked at me, then at the bed. Her head made its regular sweep towards us, and Jem said, 'Mrs Dubose, are you all right?' She did not hear him.

The alarm clock went off and scared us stiff. A minute later, nerves still tingling, Jem and I were on the sidewalk headed for home. We did not run away, Jessie sent us: before the clock wound down she was in the room pushing Jem and me out of it.

'Shoo,' she said, 'you all go home.'

Jem hesitated at the door. 'It's time for her medicine,' Jessie said. As the door swung shut behind us I saw Jessie walking quickly toward Mrs Dubose's bed.

Harper Lee

bottom plate/upper plate, false teeth
clam hole, the hole in the sand left by a clam (a sea creature with a shell in two parts, which can open and close)
Ivanhoe, a novel by Sir Walter Scott, first published in 1820
nether lip, bottom lip
tirade, long, critical speech
undulate, move like a wave
viscous, thick and sticky, between a solid and a liquid
water dippers, cups used to get water from buckets in households with no running water

The science fiction novel from which this extract is taken tells of the rise of the triffids, an intelligent species of plant that is able to move.

The Day of the Triffids

The thing would be about four feet high then. There must have been plenty of them about, growing up quietly and inoffensively, with nobody taking any particular notice of them – at least it seemed so, for if the biological or botanical experts were excited over them no news of their interest percolated to the general public. And so the one in our garden continued its growth peacefully, as did thousands like it in neglected spots all over the world.

It was some little time later that the first one picked up its roots, and walked.

That improbable achievement must, of course, have been known for some time in Russia where it was doubtless classified as a state secret, but as far as I have been able to confirm its first occurrence in the outside world took place in Indo-China – which meant that people went on taking practically no notice. Indo-China was one of those regions from which such curious and unlikely yarns might be expected to drift in, and frequently did – the kind of thing an editor might conceivably use if news were scarce and a touch of the 'mysterious East' would liven the paper up a bit. But in any case the Indo-Chinese specimen can have had no great lead. Within a few weeks reports of walking plants were pouring in from Sumatra, Borneo, Belgian Congo, Colombia, Brazil, and most places in the neighbourhood of the equator.

This time they got into print, all right. But the much-handled stories, written up with that blend of cautiously defensive frivolity which the Press habitually employed to cover themselves in matters regarding sea-serpents, elementals, thought-transference, and other irregular phenomena prevented anyone from realizing that these accomplished plants at all resembled the quiet, respectable weed beside our rubbish heap. Not until the pictures began to appear did we realize that they were identical with it save in size.

The news-reel men were quickly off the mark. Possibly they got some good and interesting pictures for their trouble of flying to outlandish places, but there was a current theory among cutters that more than a few seconds of any one news-subject – except a boxing match – could not fail to paralyse an audience with boredom. My first view, therefore, of a development which was to play such an important part in my future, as well as in so many other people's, was a glimpse sandwiched between a hula contest in Honolulu, and the First Lady launching a battleship. (That is no anachronism. They were still building them; even admirals had to live.) I was permitted to see a few triffids sway across the screen to the kind of accompaniment supposed to be on the level of the great movie-going public:

"And now, folks, get a load of what our cameraman found in Ecuador. Vegetables on vacation! *You*'ve only seen this kind of thing after a party, but down in sunny Ecuador they see it any time – and no hangover to follow! Monster plants on the march! Say, that's given me a big idea! Maybe if we can educate our potatoes right we can fix it so they'll walk right into the pot. How'd that be, Momma?"

For the short time the scene was on, I stared at it, fascinated. There was our mysterious rubbish-heap plant grown to a height of seven feet or more. There was no mistaking it – and it was 'walking'!

The bole, which I now saw for the first time, was shaggy with little rootlet hairs. It would have been almost spherical but for three bluntly-tapered projections extending from the lower part. Supported on these, the main body was lifted about a foot clear of the ground.

When it 'walked' it moved rather like a man on crutches. Two of the blunt 'legs' slid forward, then the whole thing lurched as the rear one drew almost level with them, then the two in front slid forward again. At each 'step' the long stem whipped violently back and forth: it gave one a kind of seasick feeling to watch it. As a method of progress it looked both strenuous and clumsy – faintly reminiscent of young elephants at play. One felt that if it were to go on lurching for long in that fashion it would be bound to strip all its leaves if it did not actually break its stem. Nevertheless, ungainly though it looked, it was contriving to cover the ground at something like an average walking pace.

That was about all I had time to see before the battleship launching began. It was not a lot, but it was enough to incite an investigating spirit in a boy. For, if that thing in Ecuador could do a trick like that, why not the one in our garden? Admittedly ours was a good deal smaller, but it did *look* the same....

About ten minutes after I got home I was digging round our triffid, carefully loosening the earth near it to encourage it to 'walk.'

Unfortunately there was an aspect of this self-propelled plant discovery which the news-reel people either had not experienced, or chosen for some reason of their own not to reveal. There was no warning, either. I was bending down intent on clearing the earth without harming the plant, when something from nowhere hit me one terrific slam, and knocked me out....

I woke up to find myself in bed, with my mother, my father, and the doctor watching me anxiously. My head felt as if it were split open, I was aching all over, and, as I later discovered, one side of my face was decorated with a blotchy-red raised weal. The insistent questions as to how I came to be lying unconscious in the garden were quite useless; I had no faintest idea what it was that had hit me. And some little time passed before I learned that I must have been one of the first persons in England to be stung by a triffid and get away with it. The triffid was, of course, immature. But before I had fully recovered my father had found out what had undoubtedly happened to me, and by the time I went into the garden again he had wreaked stern vengeance on our triffid, and disposed of the remains on a bonfire.

John Wyndham

anachronism, something belonging to another time
conceivably, possibly
cutters, editors
elementals, supernatural beings or forces
frivolity, silliness
incite, trigger
news-reel men, news cameramen
percolated, filtered through
ungainly, clumsy, awkward
weal, swollen mark
wreaked stern vengeance, taken hard revenge
yarns, long, rambling stories

The novel from which this extract is taken opens with a couple on a picnic, which is interrupted by a hot air balloon accident nearby.

Enduring Love

What we saw when we stood from our picnic was this: a huge grey balloon, the size of a house, the shape of a tear drop, had come down in the field. The pilot must have been half way out of the passenger basket as it touched the ground. His leg had become entangled in a rope that was attached to an anchor. Now, as the wind gusted, and pushed and lifted the balloon towards the escarpment, he was being half dragged, half carried across the field. In the basket was a child, a boy of about ten. In a sudden lull, the man was on his feet, clutching at the basket, or at the boy. Then there was another gust, and the pilot was on his back, bumping over the rough ground, trying to dig his feet in for purchase, or lunging for the anchor behind him in order to secure it in the earth. Even if he had been able, he would not have dared disentangle himself from the anchor rope. He needed his weight to keep the balloon on the ground, and the wind could have snatched the rope from his hands.

As I ran I heard him shouting at the boy, urging him to leap clear of the basket. But the boy was tossed from one side to another as the balloon lurched across the field. He regained his balance and got a leg over the edge of the basket. The balloon rose and fell, thumping into a hummock, and the boy dropped backwards out of sight. Then he was up again, arms stretched out towards the man and shouting something in return – words or inarticulate fear, I couldn't tell.

I must have been a hundred yards away when the situation came under control. The wind had dropped, the man was on his feet, bending over the anchor as he drove it into the ground. He had unlooped the rope from his leg. For some reason, complacency, exhaustion or simply because he was doing what he was told, the boy remained where he was. The towering balloon wavered and tilted and tugged, but the beast was tamed. I slowed my pace, though I did not stop. As the man straightened, he saw us – or at least the farm workers and me – and he waved us on. He still needed help, but I was glad to slow to a brisk walk. The farm labourers were also walking now. One of them was coughing loudly. But the man with the car, John Logan, knew something we didn't and kept on running. As for Jed Parry, my view of him was blocked by the balloon that lay between us.

The wind renewed its rage in the treetops just before I felt its force on my back. Then it struck the balloon which ceased its innocent comical wagging and was suddenly stilled. Its only motion was a shimmer of strain that rippled out across its ridged surface as the contained energy accumulated. It broke free, the anchor flew up in a spray of dirt, and balloon and basket rose ten feet in the air. The boy was thrown back, out of sight. The pilot had the rope in his hands and was lifted two feet clear off the ground. If Logan had not reached him and taken hold of one of the many dangling lines the balloon would have carried the boy away. Instead, both men were now being pulled across the field, and the farm workers and I were running again.

I got there before them. When I took a rope the basket was above head height. The boy inside it was screaming. Despite the wind, I caught the smell of urine. Jed Parry was on a rope seconds after me, and the two farm workers, Joseph Lacey and Toby Greene, caught hold just after him. Greene was having a coughing fit, but he kept his grip. The pilot was shouting instructions at us, but too frantically, and no one was listening. He had been struggling too long, and now he was exhausted and emotionally out of control. With five of us on the lines the balloon was secured. We simply had to keep steady on our feet and pull hand over hand to bring the basket down, and this, despite whatever the pilot was shouting, was what we began to do.

By this time we were standing on the escarpment. The ground dropped away sharply at a gradient of about twenty-five per cent, and then levelled out into a gentle slope towards the bottom. In winter this is a favourite tobogganing spot for local kids. We were all talking at once. Two of us, myself and the motorist, wanted to walk the balloon away from the edge. Someone thought the priority was to get the boy out. Someone else was calling for the balloon to be pulled down so that we could anchor it firmly. I saw no contradiction, for we could be pulling the balloon down as we moved back into the field. But the second opinion was prevailing. The pilot had a fourth idea, but no one knew or cared what it was.

I should make something clear. There may have been a vague communality of purpose, but we were never a team. There was no chance, no time. Coincidences of time and place, a predisposition to help had brought us together under the balloon. No one was in charge – or everyone was, and we were in a shouting match. The pilot, red-faced, bawling and sweating, we ignored. Incompetence came off him like heat. But we were beginning to bawl our own instructions too. I know that if I had been uncontested leader the tragedy would not have happened. Later I heard some of the others say the same thing about themselves. But there was not time, no opportunity for force of character to show. Any leader, any firm plan would have been preferable to none. No human society, from the hunter-gatherer to the post-industrial, has come to the attention of anthropologists that did not have its leaders and the led; and no emergency was ever dealt with effectively by democratic process.

Ian McEwan

accumulated, built up
anthropologists, people who study humankind
complacency, smugness, satisfaction
escarpment, a long, steep slope separating areas of land that are at different heights
hummock, little hill
predisposition, willingness, inclination

This extract is from an autobiography and describes the author's approach to bringing up his sons as a single parent.

The Boys Are Back in Town

The fact is, I run a pretty loose ship. There's a lot of give in the structure. In our world of fuzzy logic and more-or-less, we need a lot of give to get by.

It hasn't been easy eliminating the details but we've managed to work our way into a very light-handed regime: we found that the more rules we had the more crimes were created; petty prosecutions started to clog up the machinery of life. Conversely, the fewer the rules we had, the nicer we were to each other.

Fewer rules, that's the important thing, fewer but bigger rules.

It is what I like to think of as a masculine quality, the theory of outer markers. The boys have very definite limits that they mustn't go beyond. Inside the perimeter they can do very much as they please, but they must stay inside the boundaries. It's murky on the other side, they're frightened of the dark out there, I've had to see to that. But within the limits it's summertime and it's easy living. And that's what boys like – which is just as well because it's what fathers are good at: exercising a regime of benign indifference and establishing outer markers their children mustn't go beyond.

Mothers tend to a different theory. They take a more active interest in the details and the way stations through the day. Mothers like a routine; they even say that children like a routine ('It gives them security'). The bath before bedtime calms them down. This may be true, too, but in our house there aren't bedtimes, let alone baths before them.

The canon law my boys operate to is listed here in no particular order. No interrupting adults. Of course we like talking to children and we like them talking to us, but those demands for food, drink or attention that come in from nowhere, unasked, unexpected, they drive you nuts. Yes, and no swearing if you're a child not even words that sound like swearing. Except damn, of course, and hell. What else? As little stealing and lying as possible. No wanton littering, no fighting except for fun or out of earshot. Be polite as much as possible – of course, you can't when you're very angry. *You must work hard at school.* Screaming insanely, running round the house making absurd and disgusting noises, sliding in mud in the park after dark and throwing water bombs and tennis balls at windows – all these were encouraged.

But essentially, here was only one rule: they had to do what I told them. The advantage of this regime was obvious to them: I told them less – much less – than half of what two parents would tell them to do. I had also taken President Hoover's remark seriously: 'My children always obey me. And the reason is that I find out what it is they want to do and then advise them very strongly to do it.'

Not surprisingly, respectable women have found it all very under-regulated. Something must be missing, they feel. Proper homes aren't like this. It's hard to understand how my boys can be so nice without bath times. They can't understand why my boys do what they're told without complaining.

Even though their own children behave with much less respect, obedience, politeness, I feel an amused attitude to our household from a certain sort of mother. When they're pleasant about us, I'm told, they call us 'free-range'. I haven't asked what they call us when not so well-disposed. Perhaps we are 'semi-feral', perhaps we are 'feral'. Perhaps they've looked through our hedges when we're playing a summer session of garden laser hunting.

Simon Carr

benign, kindly
canon law, the standards people are judged by
feral, untamed, wild
give, flexibility
wanton, shameless
well-disposed, sympathetic, friendly

The newspaper article is about using electricity to control the mind.

'Appy ever after

"Try to relax," says Isy Goldwasser. It should be easy. I've had seven hours' sleep, coffee and eggs for breakfast. It's 10am but it's already 27ºC. I'm sitting in a picture-book-pretty converted 19th-century opera house that now serves as Goldwasser's office at the centre of Los Gatos, one of the most prosperous towns in Silicon Valley. The trouble is, Goldwasser has just attached two electrodes to my head and is about to start pumping electricity straight into my brain.

In the home of moonshots and "anything goes" optimism, the serial entrepreneur Goldwasser and his business partner, the neuroscientist Dr Jamie Tyler, are the most off-the-chart business brains you'll find. "We'll soon launch a consumer electronics product that you can use to shift your state of mind," Goldwasser assures me as he hands me the machine that controls how much electricity flows from the electrodes through my skull.

You mean hack my brain to make me feel what I want to feel, rather than what I actually do feel? I ask. "Yeah. We want to marry neuroscience and consumer electronics."

He hands me the controller. I select Calm mode. I turn the dial up and – *Holy silicon mad professors*! – it hurts. There's a sharp vibration that feels like the neurons in my head are pogoing. Not relaxing at all. I turn it down and wait. And then something remarkable happens. After a few minutes, I begin to feel waves gently flowing through my head. I don't notice at first but soon I begin to slump in my chair, my pupils dilate and my breathing slows. I really do begin to feel more relaxed. I have another go for 20 minutes and the same thing happens.

"See!" says Goldwasser, not at all calmly.

Next year Thync, Goldwasser and Tyler's company, will launch the consumer version of the product I'm testing. The two men won't go into detail because the design is still confidential. But the electrodes, which will come with a mini power pack, will be small enough to fit in the palm of your hand and be simple to attach to your head. They are likely to be controlled using a mobile phone app. You will use the app to select the mood you want to be in and determine how much current flows into your brain, using a simple slide bar. Two modes – moods – will be on offer first: calm and energy. More will follow. Thync is focusing on willpower, self-control, motivation, confidence and creativity.

Goldwasser believes harnessing willpower will have big implications in the treatment of obesity, alcoholism or gambling addiction…

Mankind has used mood-altering substances ever since we discovered alcohol, coffee and tobacco and later drugs, prescription or otherwise. Goldwasser and Tyler want to add that to the list of little helpers neuro-signalling algorithms, to give their brainwave technology its fancy name. Goldwasser, former president of the materials sciences company Symyx Technologies, and Tyler, a professor at Arizona State University, argue that "unlocking the power of the mind – regulating biology with technology – is the biggest new frontier of this century and will be one of the greatest advances of our lifetime. We're kicking it off."

Goldwasser and Tyler may sound bonkers, but if their timing is anything to go by, they're the smartest guys in the lab. Wearable gizmos are the hottest new sector in the trillion-pound global technology sector. Apple launches its first smartwatch in the new year and will be followed by wearable kit from Microsoft and Google, which promises new versions of its web-enabled spectacles, Google Glass. Many of the new devices are designed to improve our health by monitoring our blood pressure and our stress levels, keeping tabs on how much exercise we take and helping us to feel refreshed in the morning by waking us up as we are coming out of a period of deep sleep. Goldwasser and Tyler are taking the idea one step further, giving us the power to change the way we feel, whenever we want.

"Tap into your self-control. Tap into your creativity. Tap into your energy. Tap into your calm. Think of us as your third cup of coffee in the morning or your glass of wine at night," Goldwasser smiles.

John Arlidge

The Sunday Times, 30 November 2014

moonshots, ambitious projects
neurons, cells that transmit nerve signals
neuroscientist, a scientist specialising in the nervous system and the brain
neuro-signalling algorithms, processes that signal nerve pathways
pogoing, jumping up and down
regulating, controlling
serial entrepreneur, someone who keeps setting up new businesses
Silicon Valley, an area in the United States, famous for its technology businesses

This extract is taken from a 19th century text about psychology and describes the possible effects of hypnotism.

Victorian Hypnotism

Hallucinations of all the senses and delusions of every conceivable kind can be easily suggested to good subjects. You can make the subject think that he is freezing or burning, itching or covered with dirt, or wet; you can make him eat a potato for a peach, or drink a cup of vinegar for a glass of champagne; ammonia will smell to him like cologne water; a chair will be a lion, a broom-stick a beautiful woman, a noise in the street will be an orchestral music, etc., etc., with no limit except your powers of invention and the patience of the lookers on. Illusions and hallucinations form the pieces de résistance at public exhibitions. The comic effect is at its climax when it is successfully suggested to the subject that his personality is changed into that of a baby, of a street boy, of a young lady dressing for a party, of a stump orator, or of Napoleon the Great. He may even be transformed into a beast, or an inanimate thing like a chair or a carpet, and in every case will act out all the details of the part with a sincerity and intensity seldom seen at the theatre. The excellence of the performance is in these cases the best reply to the suspicion that the subject may be shamming – so skilful a shammer must long since have found his true function in life upon the stage. Hallucinations and histrionic delusions generally go with a certain depth of the trance, and are followed by complete forgetfulness. The subject awakens from them at the command of the operator with a sudden start of surprise, and may seem for a while a little dazed.

Real sensations may be abolished as well as false ones suggested. Legs and breasts may be amputated, children born, teeth extracted, in short the most painful experiences undergone, with no other anæsthetic than the hypnotizer's assurance that no pain shall be felt. Similarly morbid pains may be annihilated, neuralgias, toothaches, rheumatisms cured. The sensation of hunger has thus been abolished, so that a patient took no nourishment for fourteen days. An interesting degree of the phenomenon is found in the case related by M. Binet of a subject to whom it was suggested that a certain M. C. was invisible. She still saw M. C., but saw him as a stranger, having lost the memory of his name and his existence. – Nothing is easier than to make subjects forget their own name and condition in life. It is one of the suggestions which most promptly succeed, even with quite fresh ones. A systematized amnesia of certain periods of one's life may also be suggested, the subject placed, for instance, where he was a decade ago with the intervening years obliterated from his mind.

William James

The Principles of Psychology, 1890

amnesia, loss of memory
abolished, got rid of, stopped
ammonia, a strong-smelling gas
cologne water, eau de Cologne, perfume
delusions, false beliefs
hallucinations, things (like sounds or smells) that seem real but don't actually exist
histrionic, dramatic
intervening years, years in between
neuralgias, severe pains caused by nerve damage
pieces de résistance, showpieces, most outstanding parts
shamming, pretending
stump orator, someone who speaks passionately, in public, from a platform

This newspaper article explores the difficulties some teachers might face during their training.

OK, you try teaching 13-year-olds

Shocking news: a young trainee languages teacher on placement at Tarleton High in Lancashire "lost it" in class, barricaded the door with furniture, trapping the pupils, and threatened to kill them with something nasty that she had in her handbag. But why shocking? Imagine yourself in her place, "teaching" about 30 13- or 14-year-old creatures. Do you have one or two in your house? Are they polite, quiet and cooperative? Or are they breathtakingly insolent, noisy, crabby, offensive, skulking, smoking, drugging, and whingeing that they are not suitably entertained? What if you had 30? Wouldn't you like something in your handbag to shut the little toads up?

I'm trying not to sound bitter here, but I have taught; I have known supply-teaching hell; and I, too, have blown my top, even though it was 3.30pm and nearly over, because by then they were still climbing up walls (really), throwing scissors, dribbling glue and screaming all the while ... and when that happens, sometimes one just cannot keep one's cool a second longer.

And 13 is a particularly cruel age. In my first year's teaching, I crashed the car and sliced my forehead open on the sun-visor. Back at school, with my unsightly 27-stitch scar, I passed two 13-year-old girls. "She looks uglier than ever," said they, laughing merrily.

To be a teacher, one must be calm, sensible, tough, smartly dressed ALL THE TIME, and attractive. Otherwise, you are done for. Any degree of sensitivity can be a handicap. I blame the parents, partly. They often think teacher is a child-minding serf and their huge babies are innocent and truthful. A big mistake.

Now think of that young teacher. "She had been trying to get them to be quiet," we learn. So she had probably been shouted at and humiliated for 40 minutes. This was her very last day of several horrible weeks of a placement. The end of her torment was a whisker away, but, driven barmy by pupils, she still blew it. Her career is now ruined. But the children were "petrified ... burst into tears" and were offered "support". The pathetic little wets. She was pretending, you fools – dredging up a last desperate ploy to shut the monsters up. If she had cried, they would have laughed out loud. Hopefully, she won't be sacked. If that's what she really, really wants.

Michele Hanson

The Guardian, 21 June 2006

insolent, rude and disrespectful
ploy, cunning plan
serf, slave
wets, feeble, pathetic people

This extract is taken from a 19th century practical guide and explores the occupations available to women, one of which is to be a teacher.

Occupations Accessible to Women: Elementary Teaching

THE great difficulty of the educational question in the present day, and the obstacle to complete success in the earnest efforts made, is the difficulty, almost impossibility, of finding sufficiently-qualified teachers. The demand created by the Education Acts is estimated at over 25,000 of both sexes – the women, however, being in the majority.

The demand at present in upper-class girls' schools, and in private families, for teachers holding some kind of certificate, is quite beyond all means of supply; and amateur teachers, with no guarantee for their powers, are quite a drug in the market. Even the Government certificate, which represents the low, but thorough standard of attainment required for national schools, is much sought after; and it seems that, in future, the passing of some recognised form of examination, and the possession of some kind of a certificate, will be essential to, and ensures the success or failure of every teacher's future prospects.

Some hard study would, in some cases, be needed to supply the inaccuracy of the general style of a woman's knowledge as a very thorough grounding in elementary subjects is needful. Very few, even the most highly-educated of women, can work a sum in fractions or proportion with rapidity, much less explain every step of the process so clearly as to bring it within the comprehension of a class; and how few who write good English from habit can teach the rules of grammar correctly.

The school selected should be taught by a very good certificated master or mistress, where an assistant should be likely to learn the system of school drill and discipline, and also how practically to manage children en masse, according to the latest approved Government rules.

The duties of teachers in elementary schools are both healthful and congenial. The hours of work vary in some schools according to the season of the year, but usually the children assemble at 9:30 a.m. and are dismissed at 4:30 p.m. A quarter of an hour's run is allowed them at eleven, and an hour and a quarter (sometimes more) for dinner, thus reducing the actual school hours to five hours and a half. After school the hours are free for recreation, pleasant visits, or study.

From various authorities we find the average income of the certificated mistresses of girls' schools to be reckoned at £58, and of infant schools at £56 per annum. They live, in addition, rent free, and in some cases allowances are made for fuel, light, etc. Under the School Boards of large towns higher emoluments are offered, £75 per annum having been fixed as the minimum salary for mistresses. The comfort and advantage of possessing a small home would render the position of an elementary school-mistress an eminently tempting one to many a poor governess, could she but manage to qualify herself to hold the position.

Cassell's Household Guide, 1880s

a drug in the market, available in high numbers but no longer wanted
congenial, pleasant
drill, practice, training
emoluments, payments
en masse, as a group
proportion, work out ratios and proportions

This extract is from a 19th century practical guide and gives advice on the rearing of children.

The Rearing and Management of Children: Moral Influence – Obedience

It is commonly believed that no harm can come of letting a child have its own way, so long as it is a mere babe. But this is a serious delusion. As soon as a child is of an age to express its wants, whether by one means or another, it is old enough to be brought into habits of obedience. Obedience is the first lesson to be taught and very sensible are all well-managed babes of its meaning. No harsh words, no impatient gestures, need be added to enforce the rule, which consists simply in not doing as the babe demands, if it be not the right time and the proper place for the desired gratification.

Taking food as an example. If children were left to their own choice, they would be eating and drinking perpetually of whatever came in their way, till the stomach could no longer retain the improper substances. Wholesome food would be rejected for more palatable sweets and dainties. Before long, depraved tastes would be confirmed. Much the same misfortune sometimes befalls over-fed children of the wealthy, notwithstanding the care bestowed in other respects on their nurture; and an impaired constitution is the result. With respect to the time of feeding, irregularity should be guarded against, by not giving children scraps to eat between meals; neither should they be exposed to the sight of tempting food at unsuitable times.

Another early opportunity of implanting a spirit of obedience will be found in the impulsive habit which little children have of seizing whatever they desire to possess. This habit requires great firmness in checking, and a determination on the parent's part to risk a flood of tears rather than let the coveted article remain in the child's possession. Added to the danger which results to little children from letting this habit of snatching have sway, the destruction of property is liable to be very great.

Cassell's Household Guide, 1880s

coveted, strongly desired
dainties, good things to eat
depraved, wicked
gratification, satisfaction of a desire, indulgence
impaired constitution, poor state of health
notwithstanding, regardless of, in spite of
nurture, upbringing
palatable, tasty
perpetually, for ever
sway, strong influence or control

Practice exam paper

The Practice Exam Paper has been written to help you practise what you have learned and may not be representative of a real exam paper.

In the exam, you will be given space to write in. Here, **you will need to use your own paper for your answers**.

GCSE ENGLISH LANGUAGE

COMPONENT 1

20th Century Literature Reading and Creative Prose Writing

1 hour 45 minutes

INSTRUCTIONS

Use a black ink or black ball-point pen.

Answer **all** questions in Section A.

Select **one** title to use for your writing in Section B.

You are advised to spend your time as follows:

Section A (Reading, 40 marks)
- about 10 minutes reading
- about 50 minutes answering the questions and checking your work.

Section B (Writing, 40 marks)
- about 10 minutes planning
- about 35 minutes writing and checking your work.

SECTION A: 40 marks

*Read carefully the extract below. Then answer **all** the questions which follow it.*

Kingshaw is a schoolboy who has just found out he has to change schools. His new school is also attended by a boy called Hooper. Kingshaw knows Hooper and is frightened of him, so he has run away.

Kingshaw walked forward very cautiously into the shed, smelling his way like an animal.

It was airless and very dark. When the door swung open, a scissor of daylight fell on to the concrete floor, showing clumps of trodden-down straw, and mud. Kingshaw took another step inside, looking anxiously round him. Nothing. Nobody. A pile of old sacks in one corner. He went slowly over to them and sat down. He was shivering a little.

Seconds later, the door slammed shut. Kingshaw leaped up and ran forward, but as he put his hand out to the door, he heard the click of the padlock. After that, silence.

For a moment or two, he waited. Then he said, 'Hooper?'

Silence.

'Look, I know it's you.'

Silence.

He raised his voice. 'I can get out of here, you needn't think I'm bothered if you've locked the stupid door. I know a way to get out any time I like.'

Silence.

If Hooper had locked him in, then he had been watching out of a window, and then followed him. He was cunning, he could do anything. Yet he had seen and heard nothing, and he had kept on looking back.

He thought, perhaps it isn't Hooper.

The allotment led towards a thick hedge, and then into the fields. It was right away from the village, there never seemed to be anyone up here. But now there might be. Last year, someone had been strangled to death twenty miles away. Hooper had told him that. Twenty miles wasn't far.

He imagined tramps and murderers, and the cowman at Barr Farm, with bad teeth and hands like raw red meat. Anybody might have been hanging about behind the shed, and locked him in. Later, they might come back.

Sometimes, they were not allowed to see the newspapers, at school, because of things like murder trial reports, but they had them all in the Senior Library, and Lower School boys got sent in there, on messages. If you began to read something, your eyes went on and on, you couldn't stop them until you knew every terrible thing about it, and then you had thoughts and nightmares, you could never return to the time of not-knowing.

He remembered that he was not going back to his own school. That was all finished. He went about the building in his mind, thinking about the smells inside all the rooms. Perhaps he didn't mind so much about the people, except for Devereux and Lynch. And Mr Gardner. People didn't matter. But he couldn't separate any part of it, now, it was the whole of his existence there, that jelled together in his mind, time and place and people, and the way he felt about them.

He was still standing by the door of the hut. Somebody had used it for animals, once. It smelled faintly of pig muck, and old, dried hen pellets. The walls and roof were made of corrugated metal, bolted together. There was no window, no light at all from anywhere, except for a thin line beneath the door. Kingshaw put out his hands and began to grope his way slowly round until he came to the corner with the sacks. He sat down.

Perhaps they wouldn't wait until night before they came back. Anybody could walk down the allotment and into the shed, and never be seen. They could do anything to him, in here, choke him, or hit him with an axe, or hang him, or stab him, they could get a saw and saw off both his feet and then leave him to bleed. Kingshaw stuffed his fist in his mouth, in terror. Somebody had done that, he'd read it in one of the blood-bath books Ickden had had, last term. Ickden lent them out, at 2d. for four days. Kingshaw had read it in the bogs, and wished that he could stop himself and dreaded the nights that came after.

Now, he said to himself, it's Hooper, it's Hooper, there's nobody else it could be. Hooper would be creeping through the grass, back up to the house. Then, he would just wait. Hours and hours, all day, maybe, wait until he decided it was time to let him out.

Kingshaw said aloud, 'I'm not scared of being by myself in the bloody dark.' His voice echoed.

But it was not the dark, only the thoughts which passed through his head, the pictures in front of his eyes. He remembered why he had come here, remembered Mr Hooper's face, smiling at him, that morning, over the breakfast table. 'You will be going to school with Edmund.' He knew nothing about the place, except its name. It was called Drummonds. They were the ones who knew.

The sacks at the bottom of the pile were damp, and now the damp was coming through. Kingshaw stood up. His jeans felt wet, over his behind. He went back towards the door, and lay down on his side, trying to see out. But the crack was much thinner than he'd thought, now he got down to it, he could see nothing except a faint greyness. He stayed there, pressing his ear to the cold concrete floor of the hut, and straining for the sound of movement, for footsteps. There was nothing.

Then, minutes later, the faint sound of a truck, going down the lane. Kingshaw leaped up, and began to pound and beat upon the door, and then on the corrugated walls, until they crashed and rang in his ears, to scream and yell to be let out, he thought Oh God, God, God, please let somebody come, please let somebody come down the lane, or into the garden, please, Oh God, God, God, God…

He gave up. The palms of his hand were hot and throbbing, and the skin had come off one of his knuckles. He sucked at the loose edge, tasting blood. Silence.

Hooper might have decided to leave him in the shed for ever. There was nothing and nobody who could stop him, nothing that he would not be capable of.

Eventually, Kingshaw crawled on his hands and knees back over the concrete and the mucky straw, on to the sacks. He pulled out the bottom ones, which were the dampest, and started to spread the others over the floor. He meant to lie down. He could see nothing at all, only feel clumsily at what he was doing. Then, something ran out of the sacks over his hands. He screamed, and began to beat them desperately against his trousers, terrified of what it might be. In the end, he was certain that it had gone. His fingers, when he opened them out again, were slimy and sticky.

Susan Hill

2d., two pence, in old English money
allotment, a rented piece of land for growing vegetables or flowers
bogs, toilets
hen pellets, hen food

Read lines 1–5.

A1. List **five** things you learn about the shed from these lines. **(5 marks)**

Read lines 6–18.

A2. How does the writer show Kingshaw's feelings in these lines? **(5 marks)**

You must refer to the language used in the text to support your answer.

Read lines 19–41.

A3. What impressions do you get of the setting from these lines? **(10 marks)**

You must refer to the text to support your answer.

Read lines 42–58.

A4. How does the writer create a sense of tension in these lines? **(10 marks)**

You should write about:

- what happens to build tension
- the writer's use of language to create tension
- the effects on the reader.

Read lines 59–80.

A5. "In the last 80 or so lines of this extract, the writer encourages the reader to see Kingshaw as cowardly."

To what extent do you agree with this view? **(10 marks)**

You should write about:

- your own impressions of Kingshaw as he is presented here and in the extract as a whole
- how the writer has created these impressions.

You must refer to the text to support your answer.

SECTION B: 40 marks

In this section you will be assessed for the quality of your creative prose writing skills.

24 marks are awarded for communication and organisation; 16 marks are awarded for vocabulary, sentence structure, spelling and punctuation.

You should aim to write about 450–600 words.

Choose **one** of the following titles for your writing: **(40 marks)**

Either, (a) Taking a Chance.

Or, (b) The Secret.

Or, (c) Write about a time when you were at an exciting place.

Or, (d) Write a story which begins:

I had no idea it would end like this…

The space below can be used to plan your work.

Practice exam paper

The Practice Exam Paper has been written to help you practise what you have learned and may not be representative of a real exam paper.

In the exam, you will be given space to write in. Here, **you will need to use your own paper for your answers**.

GCSE ENGLISH LANGUAGE

COMPONENT 2

19th and 21st Century Non-Fiction Reading and Transactional/Persuasive Writing

2 hours

ADDITIONAL MATERIALS

Resource Material for use with Section A

INSTRUCTIONS

Use a black ink or black ball-point pen.

Answer **all** questions in Sections A and B.

You are advised to spend your time as follows:

Section A (Reading, 40 marks)
- about 10 minutes reading
- about 50 minutes answering the questions and checking your work.

Section B (Writing, 40 marks)
- spend about 30 minutes on each question:
  - about 5 minutes planning
  - about 25 minutes writing and checking your work.

SECTION A: 40 marks

Answer all of the following questions.

The separate Resource Material for use with Section A includes:
- *a newspaper article, 'The extraordinary story behind Danny Boyle's 127 Hours', by Patrick Barkham*
- *an extract from a diary, 'A Voyage of Discovery and Research in the Southern and Antarctic Regions, during the years 1839–43', written in 1840 by Captain Sir James Clark Ross.*

To answer the following questions, you will need to read the newspaper article by Patrick Barkham in the separate Resource Material.

A1. (a) For how long was Ralston trapped by the boulder? **(1 mark)**
(b) How much water did Ralston have with him? **(1 mark)**
(c) How much did the rock that trapped him weigh? **(1 mark)**

A2. Patrick Barkham is trying to persuade us to watch the film *127 hours*.
How does he try to do this? **(10 marks)**

You should comment on:
- what he says to influence readers
- his use of language and tone
- the way he presents his review.

To answer the following questions, you will need to read the extract by Captain Sir James Clark Ross in the separate Resource Material.

A3. (a) What does the writer mean by 'weathered the breeze' in line 3? **(1 mark)**
(b) What does the writer say was made possible due to the favourable weather? **(2 marks)**

A4. What do you think and feel about James Clark Ross's description of the disaster he faced at sea? **(10 marks)**

You should comment on:
- what is said
- how it is said.

You must refer to the text to support your comments.

To answer the following questions, you will need to use both texts.

A5. According to these two writers, what is dangerous about the situations in which they find themselves? **(4 marks)**

A6. Both of these texts are about the way men deal with disaster. Compare the following:
- the writers' attitudes to disaster
- how they express their ideas about disaster. **(10 marks)**

You must use the text to support your comments and make it clear which text you are referring to.

SECTION B: 40 marks

Answer Question B1 **and** *Question B2.*

In this section you will be assessed for the quality of your writing skills.

For each question, 12 marks are awarded for communication and organisation; 8 marks are awarded for vocabulary, sentence structure, punctuation and spelling.

Think about the purpose and audience for your writing.

You should aim to write about 300–400 words for each task.

B1. A local company is keen to understand the possible dangers their Australian Surf and Diving adventure holiday packages might present.

Write a report for the Managing Director of the company suggesting what dangers may be involved.

You could include:
- examples of the dangers that may be involved
- your ideas about how to make this holiday package as safe as possible. **(20 marks)**

B2. A proposal has been made to ban all cyclists from your town centre in an effort to reduce the number of road traffic accidents.

You have decided to write an article for your local newspaper to share your views on this proposal. You could write in favour of or against this proposal.

Write a lively article for the newspaper giving your views. **(20 marks)**

Danny Boyle's new film, 127 Hours, tells how climber Aron Ralston found himself trapped alone in a canyon and had to perform DIY surgery to save his life.

The extraordinary story behind Danny Boyle's 127 Hours

For six days, Aron Ralston kept himself alive with fierce self-control and a conviction that only logical thought could let him survive. But the epiphany when the 27-year-old climber realised how he could save his own life came from an explosion of blind rage.

Ralston had been climbing the narrow canyons of Utah alone when a dislodged boulder fell on to his right arm, trapping him against a rock. He was entombed in the wilderness of Bluejohn Canyon, carrying a small rucksack with just one litre of water, two burritos and a few chunks of chocolate. He had headphones and a video camera but no mobile phone – and there was no reception anyway. Most foolishly of all, he had not told anyone where he was going. He eked out his water, futilely chipping away at the 800lb rock and slowly entering a state of delirium, until he was eventually forced to cut off his trapped arm, with the small knife from his cheap multitool kit.

When his blunt knife pierced his skin but came to rest against solid bone, Ralston thought there was no chance he could perform the gruesome amputation that would save his life. He brushed some grit from his trapped thumb and a sliver of flesh peeled off "like the skin of boiled milk", he remembers. "I'm like, what the . . . ? I take my knife and I'm poking a bit more and the knife just slips into the meat of my thumb like it's going into room-temperature butter. My hand has almost jellified. The knife tip goes in and, 'pssstt', the gases from decomposition escape and there's this putrid smell. I go into this rage. I'm in this hyper-emotional state after all this regimented discipline to keep it together and in this moment, when I'm trying to rip my arm out from the rock, I feel it bend and it stops me – 'That's it! I can use the boulder to break my bones!' "

The year before his accident, Ralston quit his job as an engineer with Intel to climb all Colorado's "fourteeners" – its peaks over 14,000ft. In May 2003, he began "canyoneering" in Utah, navigating the narrow passages of Bluejohn with a mixture of free-climbing, daring jumps and climbing with ropes. He was negotiating a 10ft drop in a 3ft-wide canyon listening to his favourite band, Fish, when he dislodged a boulder he thought was stable. "I go from being out on a lark in a beautiful place and just being so happy and carefree to, like, oh shit. I fell a few feet, in slow motion, I look up and the boulder is coming and I put my hands up and try to push myself away and it collides and crushes my right hand." Ralston was pinned in the canyon, his right hand and lower arm crushed by the 800lb rock. "There was this stunned moment of what-?" he laughs. "And it's almost comic."

The next second, the pain struck. "If you've ever crushed your finger in a door accidentally," he says, this was "times 100". In an "adrenalised rage", for 45 minutes he "cursed like a pirate". Then he reached for his water bottle. As he drank, he had to force himself to stop. "I realise this water is the only thing that's going to keep myself alive," he says. Having failed to tell anyone where he was going, he knew he would not be found. "I put the lid back on the water bottle and gathered myself. It was like, all right, brut going to do it. This is the stop-think-observe-plan phase of rational problem-solving. I have to think my way out of here." As he describes how he thought through his options, he taps his prosthetic arm on his fingers.

He ruled out the most drastic option – suicide – but the next most drastic alternative came to him immediately. "There's this surreal conversation with myself. 'Aron, you're gonna have to cut your arm off.' 'I don't want to cut my arm off!' 'Dude, you're gonna have to cut your arm off.' I said it to myself. That little back-and-forth. Then, 'Wait a minute. Stop. I'm not talking to myself. That's just crazy. You're not talking to yourself, Aron.' Except I would continue to talk to myself in various ways, to remind myself not to pass out."

After two days spent fruitlessly chipping away at the rock with his knife and devising a clever but futile system of pulleys with his climbing clips and ropes to hoist the boulder clear – he was defeated because climbing rope is stretchy and he couldn't obtain the required tension – he put his knife to his arm, only to find it was so blunt he couldn't even cut his body hair.

The next morning, finally, came the rage and its revelation – that Ralston could fling himself against the boulder to break his own bones. From then, it was easy. The snap of his bones "like, pow!" was a horrifying sound "but to me it was euphoric", he recalls. "The detachment had already happened in my mind – it's rubbish, it's going to kill you, get rid of it Aron. It's an 'it'. It's no longer my arm. As I picked up the knife, I was very cool and collected." It took him an hour to hack through his flesh. "As painful as it all was, the momentum of the euphoria was driving it," he says.

Patrick Barkham

The Guardian, 15 December 2010

Bluejohn, a canyon in Utah
Colorado, a state in the USA
conviction, belief
decomposition, decay, rotting
delirium, madness
eked out, made (it) last longer
entombed, buried
epiphany, inspiration, realisation
euphoric, euphoria, intensely happy, intense happiness
futilely, futile, pointlessly, pointless
lark, adventure
putrid, rotten
surreal, bizarre
Utah, a state in the USA

This extract is from a diary entry written in 1840 by a captain of a ship.

A Voyage of Discovery and Research in the Southern and Antarctic Regions

July 1840

During the night the wind and sea subsided, and we had a comparatively fine morning. We were all anxiously looking out for the Terror, and wondering how she had weathered the breeze, when a wooden hoop of a cask was seen close to us. By this we felt certain that she had run past us during the time that we were hove-to for her, and was now probably far ahead; we therefore pressed all sail on the ship to endeavour to overtake her. The day being very favourable, we seized the opportunity of drying our sails and clothes, which had been most thoroughly drenched, and of repairing the damages we had sustained.*

In this and many other respects we felt the fine weather to be a great advantage to us; but this afternoon it pleased God to visit us by an unlooked-for calamity, – Mr. Roberts, the boatswain, whilst engaged about the rigging, fell overboard and was drowned. The life-buoy was instantly let go, and two boats lowered down; they reached the spot where we saw him sink only a few seconds too late! The gloom which the loss of one of our small party, at the outset of our voyage, occasioned, was for a time merged in feelings of painful anxiety, and afterwards of heartfelt gratitude, for the merciful preservation of the whole crew of one of the boats, who in their humane endeavours to save the life of our unfortunate shipmate, very nearly sacrificed their own. Mr. Oakley, mate, and Mr. Abernethy, the gunner, had returned to the ship with one boat, when the other, still at a considerable distance from us, was struck by a sea, which washed four of the crew out of her. Mr. Abernethy immediately again pushed off from the ship, and succeeded in saving them from their perilous situation, completely benumbed and stupefied with the cold. The boats were, with much difficulty, owing to the sea that was running, hoisted up, and not until after one of them had been again swamped alongside.

We resumed our course under all sail, although this calamitous detention of some hours frustrated all our expectations of overtaking the Terror. A small iceberg, seen at a considerable distance just before dark, warned us to be vigilant during the night, which at this season being fifteen hours long obliged us to run at all hazards, or to delay our voyage to a ruinous extent. It has at all times a good effect upon those whose duty it is to look out, and an advantageous stimulus even to the most diligent, occasionally to see real dangers; but they were, in this instance, the cause of several false alarms, from the impression left upon our minds.

July 31

The weather continued fine all night and the greater part of the next day. Numerous birds of the petrel kind, which were flying about, seemed to enjoy the short-lived tranquillity, and were eagerly employed searching the patches of floating sea-weed for small fish and marine insects, which find a precarious security amongst its densely interwoven branches from the persecutions of their enemies.

**The Terror – another ship.*

Captain Sir James Clark Ross

boatswain, a ship's officer in charge of equipment and crew
calamity, calamitous, disaster, disastrous
cask, barrel
detention, delay
endeavour, endeavours, attempt, attempts
hove-to, stopped
humane, kind
precarious, uncertain
preservation, keeping safe
stupefied, shocked

Answers

SECTION A: READING

1. Planning your exam time

1 10 minutes
2 About 6 minutes (Note: You could choose to spend a total of 5 minutes (1 minute per mark) to save time for checking your work.)
3 Lines 20–33.
4 About $1\frac{1}{4}$ minutes (Note: You could choose to spend just 1 minute per part, to save time for checking your work.)
5 Two texts
6 All should be circled

2. Reading texts explained

1 (a) Answers provided on page 2 of Workbook
(b) For example: The use of 'pinpoint pupils' creates a sinister, frightening atmosphere.
2 (a) Some hard study would, in some cases, be needed to supply the inaccuracy of the general style of a woman's knowledge as a very thorough grounding in elementary subjects is needful. Very few, even the most highly-educated of women, can work a sum in fractions or proportion with rapidity, much less explain every step of the process so clearly as to bring it within the comprehension of a class; and how few who write good English from habit can teach the rules of grammar correctly.
(b) Answers should use the evidence identified in Question 2 (a) to make the key point that the author feels women are poorly educated and ill-prepared for teaching.

3. Reading questions explained 1

1 Component 1, AO1(a): Answer provided on page 3 of Workbook
2 Component 2, A1: AO1(a)
3 Component 1, A4: AO2
4 Component 2, A3: AO1(a)
5 Component 2, A5: AO1(b)

4. Reading questions explained 2

1 (a) Component 1, A5: AO4
(b) Component 2, A4: AO4
(c) Component 2, A6: AO3
2 Only Component 1, A5 should be ticked
3 All of the extract or extracts

5. Reading the questions

1 (a) Answer provided on page 5 of Workbook
(b) 'List'
2 Component 1, A2: 1 text; lines 8–14; 'How does the writer' and 'life is like for Shukhov'; about 6 minutes
Component 1, A4: 1 text; lines 20–33; 'How does the writer create a sense of despair and hardship', 'use of language' and 'effects on the reader'; about 12 minutes
Component 2, A6: two texts; all of each text; 'teaching', 'compare', 'writers' attitudes' and 'how'; about 12 minutes
(Note: The calculation for the length of time to spend on each answer is based on $1\frac{1}{4}$ minutes per mark. You could choose to spend just 1 minute per mark to save time for checking your work.)

6. Skimming for the main idea or theme

1 (a) Answer provided on page 6 of Workbook
(b) For example: The opening sentence suggests that the main idea will be the difficulties of teaching, although it also suggests **that the article will be about why teachers find it difficult to control their anger**.
2 For example: The end of the article suggests that whilst it is the students who get support, it is the teachers who suffer the most.
3 For example: The ideas expressed at the end of the article differ from those at the beginning as the beginning of the article suggests teachers are aggressive, while the end suggests their careers can be ruined by children's poor behaviour.
4 For example: The main idea in the article is that poor behaviour in schools can make life really difficult for teachers.

7. Annotating the texts

1 Answer provided on page 7 of Workbook
2 Because annotated detail E falls outside the lines of the extract given in the question
3 Answers should include four or five annotations, for example:
- 'launching a battleship' – suggests war is being declared
- 'why not the one in our garden?' – suggests the danger is coming closer to home
- 'There was no warning, either' – gives the impression that people hadn't previously seen them as a threat
- 'no faintest idea what it was that had hit me' – suggests that the triffids' stings are very powerful and like nothing he has experienced before
- 'immature' – hints at the idea that a fully grown triffid will be far more dangerous.

8. Putting it into practice

1 (a) and (b) Answers should include four or five annotated words or phrases, for example:
- 'came under control' – suggests the worst is over
- 'wind had dropped' – suggests relief, as the threat of the power of the wind is reduced
- 'towering balloon wavered and tilted and tugged' – gives the idea that the balloon is calmer but still a potential threat
- 'the beast was tamed' – suggests the situation is under control but emphasises the danger the balloon presents in the use of 'beast'
- 'though I did not stop' – 'though' hints at the idea that he may need to pick up his pace again soon.

2 For example: The impression given of the rescue in these lines is that the danger has passed. The reader is told that the situation is 'under control' and that the 'wind had dropped', which suggests relief that the worst is now over. This idea is echoed in the phrase 'the beast was tamed'.
However, these lines also provide hints that this sense of control and relief may only be temporary. For example, the reader learns that the 'towering balloon wavered and tilted and tugged', suggesting that, while it is currently calm, it may rise up again at any moment. This is supported by the metaphor 'beast', which reinforces the idea of the balloon as a wild thing that, in fact, cannot be tamed.

9. Putting it into practice

1 (a) and (b) Answers should include four or five annotated words or phrases, for example:
- 'a pretty loose ship' – suggests lack of rules and discipline
- 'petty prosecutions' – suggests the writer doesn't feel that the majority of children's bad behaviour is worthy of punishment
- 'outer markers' – suggests the writer approaches parenting like a sport
- 'Mothers like a routine' – gives the idea that the writer disagrees with these mothers and takes a different approach
- 'respectable women have found it all very under-regulated' – reinforces the idea that the writer prefers his own approach.

2 For example: Simon Carr has a relaxed attitude to bringing up children. For example, he admits that he runs 'a pretty loose ship', which might imply a lack of rules and discipline. Moreover, the reference to 'petty prosecutions' gives the impression that Carr does not feel that most of his children's bad behaviour deserves to be punished. These ideas are supported by the use of sports terminology such as 'outer markers', which suggests that Carr approaches parenting as if it were a game or sport.
Carr recognises that there are other approaches to parenting and his reference to how 'mothers like a routine' suggests that he disagrees with the idea of a routine and chooses not to follow one. This sense that the writer prefers his own approach is reinforced when he says 'respectable women have found it all very under-regulated'.

10. Explicit information and ideas

1 (a) Answer provided on page 10 of Workbook
(b) Los Gatos
(c) 27°C

2 For example: Writing in full sentences, or copying long phrases, will waste time in the exam. It is only necessary to use the shortest possible quotation when giving explicit information.

3 (a) Tarleton High
(b) 13
(c) 27

11. Implicit ideas

1
- The hammer is used to wake them up. – Answer provided on page 11 of Workbook
- They have to get up at five o'clock. – Explicit
- The windows are covered with thick ice. – Answer provided on page 11 of Workbook
- The sun is not yet up. – Implicit
- It is very cold. – Answer provided on page 11 of Workbook

2 Answers should include four implicit ideas, for example:
- Conditions are over-crowded.
- There is no adequate bedding to keep them warm.
- They have no proper toilet facilities.
- Their boots are usually worn wet.

12. Inference

1 Annotations could include:
- 'I didn't look any more than I had to.'
- 'Mrs Dubose would catch him'
- 'anywhere to keep from looking at her'

2 For example:
(a) The extract suggests that Mrs Dubose is **frightening, as the sentence, 'I didn't look any more than I had to' gives the impression that the narrator is scared of her.**
(b) The phrase 'Mrs Dubose would catch him' creates the idea that Mrs Dubose is fierce and someone to be wary of.

3 For example:
Mrs Dubose's house seems intimidating from the start of the extract, as it has 'steep front steps'. The house also frightens the children as they are met by an 'oppressive odour', which makes the narrator 'afraid, expectant' and 'watchful'. The odour is described as something usually smelt in 'rain-rotted' houses, which gives the reader the impression that the house **is old, uncared for and possibly unsafe. There is also a suggestion that the house is unclean when the writer uses the description 'unbleached domestic sheets'. It seems clear that the house is not a pleasant place to be as the reader is told that the narrator feels 'afraid, expectant, watchful'.**
This sense of intimidation and fear continues with the introduction of Mrs Dubose. She initially seems vulnerable as she is described as 'lying under a pile of quilts', and the descriptions of the 'glass with a teaspoon' and the 'ear syringe' suggest she may be unwell. However, the phrases 'for a moment' and 'almost friendly' indicate that Mrs Dubose may not be welcoming and this is reinforced in her first, hostile words, when she describes the narrator as 'dirty'.

13. Interpreting information and ideas

1 (a) 'thorough grounding' – Answer provided on page 13 of Workbook
(b) 'with rapidity' – Answer provided on page 13 of Workbook
(c) 'comprehension of a class' – understanding of the class (of children)
(d) 'certificated' – qualified
(e) 'school drill' – school rules

2 Manage a large number of children at the same time

3 (a) They are trying very hard.
(b) That it is extremely difficult to recruit enough well-qualified teachers, particularly women.

14. Point – Evidence – Explanation

1 Evidence B

2 Evidence B is the most effective because it is an example of a list of adjectives and therefore links directly to the point made.

3 Evidence: For example, she uses the words [for example] **'barricaded', 'trapping' and 'threatened'.**
Explanation B

4 For example: Explanation B is more effective because it is fully developed and more specific, suggesting that the teacher treated the children like prisoners. The word 'also' signals additional details, which explore the teacher's actions further.

15. Putting it into practice

1 A1. For example:
(a) They grew quietly without drawing attention to themselves.
(b) Nobody took any notice of them.
(c) Scientific experts were excited about them.
(d) The public had no knowledge about the triffids.
(e) They grew in neglected spots.

2 A3. Answers could include these key points:

- the triffids attracted a lot of press attention and news people 'were quickly off the mark', which suggests they were initially viewed as a new type of sport
- news people fly to 'outlandish places', which suggests excitement
- 'sandwiched between a hula contest' and jokes such as 'educate our potatoes' give the impression they are not taken seriously
- hyperbole and alliteration are used in the news announcement 'Vegetables on vacation!', suggesting the triffids are viewed as comical and harmless
- 'hangover' indicates there is a party atmosphere in response to the triffids
- the narrator is 'fascinated'
- the exclamation mark after 'walking' suggests ordinary people are becoming excited.

16. Putting it into practice

1 A2. Answers could include these key points:

- Use of fact – 'a young trainee languages teacher on placement at Tarleton High', '27-stitch scar'
- Use of opinion – '13 is a particularly cruel age', 'supply-teaching hell'
- Use of expert evidence – 'I have taught', 'I passed two 13-year-old girls…'
- Rhetorical questions to persuade – 'Wouldn't you like something in your handbag…?'
- Use of verbs with connotations of violence to emphasise what teachers are driven to – 'barricaded', 'trapping', 'threatened'
- Colloquial language to create sarcasm – 'lost it', 'blown my top', 'blew it'
- Language to present the students as weak and to minimise the teacher's reaction – 'little toads', 'huge babies', 'pathetic little wets'
- Use of lists to reinforce points – the character of the students ('insolent, noisy, crabby, offensive…') and what a teacher needs to be to succeed ('calm, sensible, tough, smartly dressed…').

17. Word classes

1
- Noun – for example, 'furniture', 'handbag'
- Verb – Answer provided on page 17 of Workbook
- Adverb – Answer provided on page 17 of Workbook
- Adjective – for example, 'insolent', 'noisy'

2 For example: The lists of adjectives build up contrasting pictures in a reader's mind of what teenagers are like. For instance, 'polite, quiet and co-operative' creates a positive image, whilst 'insolent, noisy, crabby…' creates a negative image. This will make the reader question their own view of teenagers.

3 For example:

(a) The action verb 'dig' suggests very hard physical labour, which reinforces the hardships of the labour camp in the mind of the reader.

(b) The verb 'run' is effective because it reminds the reader that the prisoners are unable to run away and that there is no escape.

18. Connotations

1 (a) outer markers – border, sport
perimeter – extreme edge, limits, outskirts
boundaries – cricket pitch, limits, dividing line

(b) For example: While the words 'outer markers', 'perimeter' and 'boundaries' suggest that the writer sees parenting as a sport, they also indicate that he does give his children limits and that they have to pay attention to these limits.

2 For example:

(a) The adjective 'rain-rotted' has connotations of neglect and decay, and suggests that Mrs Dubose's house might also be old, crumbling and worn.

(b) The 'coal-oil lamps' have old-fashioned connotations and give the impression of a dark, smoky space.

19. Figurative language

1 For example:
The writer uses the simile 'like a glacier', which has connotations of **icy cold, arctic conditions and something that is hard, sharp and dangerous.** This suggests to the reader **that Mrs Dubose is cold, harsh and unfriendly.**

2 For example:
The simile 'like a clam hole at low tide' suggests a wide, dirty opening. This gives the reader an impression of Mrs Dubose that is foul and unattractive.
The suggestion in the simile 'like some viscous substance coming to a boil' is that Mrs Dubose is capable of hurting others with what she says.

3 Mrs Dubose is presented as repulsive and frightening in appearance. For example, the metaphor 'cords of saliva' suggests that thick strands of saliva cover her mouth. This presents her to the reader as unhuman and creates a frightening vision of her mouth as something dangerous.

20. Creation of character

1 The writer uses dialogue to show that Mrs Dubose is rude as she calls Jem's sister 'dirty'. However, Jem's dialogue shows that he is **brave and 'quietly' able to stand up to Mrs Dubose, even if his defiant words 'I ain't scared of you' suggest that he may be a little more afraid than he is letting on. His words also show that he is protective of his sister when he contradicts Mrs Dubose, saying that she 'ain't dirty'.**

2 Answers could include these key points:
- 're-opened' suggests that Jem is not intimidated by Mrs Dubose
- 'read too fast' and 'skipped' suggest he is reckless as he is trying to fool Mrs Dubose
- 'dangling in mid-air' suggests he is brave.

3 Answers could include these key points:
- Description – a very detailed, unattractive image of Mrs Dubose is built up through:
  - figurative language – such as 'like a glacier', 'cords of saliva', 'like a clam hole at low tide', 'like some viscous substance coming to a boil'
  - carefully chosen adjectives – such as 'horrible', 'dirty', 'pinpoint', 'knobby'
- Action – Mrs Dubose's actions suggest she is, for example:
  - physically unattractive – 'she would draw her nether lip to her upper plate and carry her chin with it'
  - harsh and a little cruel – 'catch him and make him'.

21. Creating atmosphere

1 For example:
'rage' – uncontrollable force, suggests the wind is violent
'force'– suggests strength and violence
'struck' – hurt, damage, suggests the wind is a weapon

2 For example:
Action verbs – 'struck', 'broke', 'flew', 'rose'
Personification (of the balloon) – 'innocent comical wagging'
Adjectives – 'innocent', 'comical', 'ridged'

3 (a) Answer extract B
(b) For example: Answer extract B is the most effective as it uses a clear P-E-E structure and fully explains the connotations of 'rage' and 'force'.

4 For example: Overall, the writer creates an atmosphere of **tension and danger by personifying the wind and describing in detail the actions of the rescuers.**

22. Narrative voice

1 Extract 1: A
Extract 2: C
Extract 3: B

2 Answers could include these key points about the first-person narration:
- shows how scornful he is of others – 'Incompetence came off him like heat'
- shows his complete confidence in his own ability – 'the tragedy would not have happened'.

23. Putting it into practice

1 Answers could include these key points:
- overall – build-up of action using strong verbs, together with vivid picture of the balloon creates drama and tension
- description of the balloon emphasises scale of problem – 'the size of a house'
- imagery for the balloon – 'the shape of a teardrop'
- personification of the balloon, and use of strong and action verbs, emphasises the scale of the problem – 'gusted', 'pushed' and 'lifted'
- verbs used for the rescuers' actions suggest desperation and a battle with the balloon – 'clutching', 'bumping', 'trying', 'lunging', 'snatched' (which also has connotations of stealing, running away with)
- verbs used to highlight the power of the wind and the balloon – 'tossed from one side to another' makes the boy seem helpless, like a rag doll.

24. Putting it into practice

1 Answers could include these key points:
- overall – life is monotonous and harsh
- 'Ah, but not simply to report as usual' – emphasises the monotony, routine
- 'fate' – has negative connotations, suggests life will get worse in the camp
- 'shift' – verb suggests the men are pushed around like objects
- action verbs suggesting hard manual labour – 'put up posts', 'dig' are followed by 'start building', which suggests relentless work
- 'not a dog kennel' – creates vivid picture that suggests harsh conditions and that the men are treated like animals
- 'covered with snow drifts' – reinforces the harsh, cold conditions

25. Rhetorical devices 1

1 For example, four of:
- pattern of three – 'polite, quiet and cooperative'
- lists – 'insolent, noisy, crabby, offensive, …'
- alliteration – 'skulking, smoking'
- rhetorical questions – 'But why shocking?'
- colloquial language –'lost it', 'whingeing', 'shut the little toads up'.

2 For example (taking the example of colloquial language): … The writer also uses **colloquial language at the start of the article when she states that the teacher 'lost it' in class. The writer uses this conversational tone to suggest that the teacher behaved like a teenager. As this phrase is used by young people to describe losing control, it will encourage readers to make a negative judgement about the teacher.**

26. Rhetorical devices 2

1 For example: The repetition of 'Mothers' at the start of two sentences is a little sarcastic as it seems to mock their importance. The writer then repeats the word 'routine' to emphasise the way mothers rely on rules. This makes routines sound petty, particularly as it is followed by humorous comments that show the writer has no routine whatsoever in his house.

2 For example: The words 'no particular order' suggest there is no routine in the writer's household, that all rules are equal and they can be applied at any time. This contrasts with the bedtime routine preferred by mothers, where there is a clear structure, which in turn emphasises the writer's relaxed attitude to parenting.

3 For example: Hyperbole: The phrase 'Except damn, of course, and hell' is used to add humour as it exaggerates the unusual rules the writer has put in place.
Emotive language: The emotive language in 'Screaming insanely' is used to build a picture for the reader of a fun and relaxed household.

27. Fact, opinion and expert evidence

1 (a) A
(b) C
(c) B

2 For example: The writer feels that teaching is made very difficult by poorly behaved children.

3 Fact: 'my… 27-stitch scar'
Opinion: 'supply-teaching hell', '13 is a particularly cruel age'
Expert evidence: 'I passed two 13-year-old girls. "She looks uglier than ever," said they, laughing merrily.'

4 For example:
Fact: The writer includes the fact about the number of stitches to emphasise the cruelty of the girls given the serious nature of her injury.
Opinion: The writer gives her opinion that supply teaching is 'hell' to reinforce the extent of the challenge faced by teachers.
Expert evidence: The writer's own story about the rude 13-year-old girls makes her view that children are poorly behaved seem believable as it comes from an actual experience of behaviour in schools.

28. Identifying sentence types

1 A: single-clause sentence
B: multi-clause sentence (subordinate)
C: multi-clause sentence (coordinate)
D: minor

2 For example:
Single-clause: 'Her career is now ruined.'
Multi-clause (subordinate): 'If she had cried, they would have laughed out loud.'
Multi-clause (coordinate): ' But the children were "petrified ... burst into tears" and were offered "support".'
Minor: 'The pathetic little wets.'

29. Commenting on sentence types

1 For example: The series of quicker, short sentences at the beginning of the extract suggests an initial atmosphere of tension and fear. The longer, multi-clause sentence slows the extract down and reflects the new sense of calm in the scene being described.

2 For example:
The writer starts the paragraph with a short, single-clause sentence **and the next few sentences are similarly short. These are used to present the basic facts of the scene and leave the reader wanting more details.**
After using short sentences, the writer then uses a multi-clause sentence. This adds to the tension **because the structure of the sentence builds up the sense of danger and keeps the reader waiting for the climax of the rescue.**
The writer then uses two multi-clause sentences that end with subordinate clauses. This adds to the tension **as the first multi-clause sentence suggests bravery, while the second increases the sense of anticipation by delaying the most worrying information until the final clause.**

30. Structure: non-fiction

1 For example: Hanson starts her article by shocking readers with a vivid and detailed description of a teacher who 'lost it' in class. Readers will want to read on to find out the rest of the story, and to find out how Hanson really feels about teachers.

2 Warnings – Hanson wants readers to think carefully about behaviour in the classroom, and the effects this could have on teachers' careers.

3 For example:
Initially, Arlidge is scared about the idea of having two electrodes attached to his head. This is implied in the phrase 'pumping electricity straight into my brain'. However, when he actually tries the electrodes, his tone changes. **This is signalled in the short sentence 'And then something remarkable happens', which draws attention to a shift in his reaction to what is happening. This is then followed by two longer sentences creating a positive picture of 'waves gently flowing', which reflect his calmer state of mind. The verb 'slump' contrasts with the earlier verb 'pumping' and suggests a complete change in mood.**

31. Structure: fiction

1 For example:
The underlined sentences show that the balloon is already out of control and that the pilot is in difficulty. This suggests to the reader that the danger ahead will be far greater as they will not be able to rely on the pilot for experienced help.

2 For example:
The writer withholds the fact that there is a boy in the basket as this structure increases the tension for the reader. Before this fact is revealed, the writer closely describes **the balloon, using the similes 'the size of a house' and 'the shape of a teardrop' to give the reader an idea of the scale of the crisis. The personification of the wind in 'pushed and lifted' also builds tension by highlighting its power.**
The revelation that there is a boy in the basket increases the tension because **readers already know the pilot is tangled up in the rope and that the balloon is out of control. The tension is also increased by the mention of the boy's young age in the final part of sentence.**

3 Answers should include comments about the writer's use of closely described detail and action, which emphasise the length of time the rescue takes and how difficult it is.

32. Putting it into practice

1 Answers could include these key points:
- sounds exciting – 'trick like that'; sentence ends with use of ellipsis...
- use of ellipsis at ends of paragraphs creates cliffhangers
- short paragraph ('About ten minutes after...') continues the excited tone, then 'Unfortunately' at the beginning of the next paragraph suggests a change in tone
- closely described detail of the narrator's actions draws out the sense of tension
- short sentence ('there was no warning') creates suspense.

33. Putting it into practice

1 Answers could include these key points.
Language:
- use of facts (for example, 'Mankind has used mood-altering substances ever since we discovered alcohol...') make the article more believable and opinions (for example, 'the most off-the-chart business brains') show that the writer feels that these people should be admired
- use of expert evidence throughout (for example, 'Goldwasser assures me') makes the writer sound reliable, as does the later information about the experts' backgrounds and qualifications
- hyperbole ('pumping electricity' and 'hack my brain') exaggerates the writer's fear for comic effect
- lists ('willpower, self-control, motivation, confidence and creativity') suggest the mind-altering technique could have many helpful uses
- repetition ('tap into') makes technique sound very positive and enjoyable.

Structure:
- starts by hinting at writer's fear ('Try to relax'), to make readers want to find out what exactly has frightened him
- change in tone ('And then something remarkable happens') entertains as it shows surprise that technique works
- variety of sentence structures is used to suggest writer is nervous when the electricity is turned on.

34. Handling two texts

1 separate
2 Assessment objective 3
3 (a) Component 2
(b) Question A6
(c) Question A5
(d) Question A5
(e) Question A6
(f) Question A6
(g) Question A5

35. Selecting evidence for synthesis

1 According to these <u>two writers</u>, what are the <u>positive aspects of mind-altering techniques</u>?
2 (a) (i); (b) (i)
3 For example, from *The Boys Are Back in Town*:
- mothers 'take a more active interest in the details'
- 'Mothers like a routine'
- 'The bath before bedtime calms them down'.

For example, from 'The Rearing and Management of Children':
- 'simply in not doing as the babe demands'
- 'Obedience is the first lesson to be taught'
- 'With respect to the time of feeding, irregularity should be guarded against'.

36. Synthesising evidence

1 **Similarly**, likewise, **both writers feel, in the same way**, both texts suggest
2 For example: You should use adverbials and linking phrases in your synthesis of evidence to link together the similarities you find between the two texts.
3 (a) Overview C
(b) For example: Overview C shows an understanding of the specific similarity between the two texts.
4 Answers should use suitable adverbials and linking phrases and start with the overview identified in Question 3 (a). They could also use the evidence identified for Question 3 on page 35.
For example: Both writers feel that mind-altering techniques can have a positive impact on health and happiness. For instance, Arlidge quotes an expert who feels that mind-altering techniques can have an impact on the treatment of 'obesity, alcoholism' and 'gambling addiction'. Similarly, 'Victorian Hypnotism' stresses the health benefits of mind-altering techniques as the writer feels that hypnotism can allow 'the most painful experiences' to be endured without any anaesthetic.

37. Looking closely at language

1 'bonkers' – Answer provided on page 37 of Workbook
'gizmos' – means 'modern gadgets', an informal term with trendy connotations
'wearable kit' – suggests fashionable and essential, rather than functional, items
2 For example: The colloquial language of 'bonkers', meaning 'mad' or 'crazy', creates an informal tone with positive connotations. The word 'gizmos' and the phrase 'wearable kit' both suggest fashionable items rather than functional ones, which creates the impression that the writer does not really take the new technology seriously.
3 For example: The three subordinate clauses contain more factual information about the purpose of the devices, such as 'monitoring our blood pressure'. This gives the sentence a more serious and scientific tone.
4 (a) For example: The repetition of 'tap into' makes changing the way we feel sound simple.
(b) For example: The long sentence that follows the repetition in the four short sentences creates a reassuring effect, which persuades the reader that this is something they might want to try.

38. Planning to compare

1 Completed plans should include example quotations and explanations.
For example, for Extract 1:
Tone – formal language, for example 'The duties of teachers', 'The hours of work' – suggests order and authority
Rhetorical devices/language – formal language, for example 'free for recreation' – gives a positive image of life for teachers
Sentences – longer sentences with subordinate clauses deliver a lot of detail, which adds to the authoritative tone

39. Comparing ideas

1 (a) Both texts start by expressing ideas about **problems in the education system.**
(b) Hanson feels **that the main problem is the behaviour of students in the classroom** whereas 'Occupations Accessible to Women' **suggests that the biggest difficulty is the lack of suitably qualified teachers.**
2 Text 1: Supply teaching is very challenging – 'supply-teaching hell'
Text 2: Teaching is a rewarding and pleasant profession – 'The duties of teachers in elementary schools are both healthful and congenial'
3 For example: Both texts focus on the nature of teaching and its effect on teachers. Hanson uses hyperbole to argue that supply teaching is very challenging as she calls it 'supply-teaching hell'. On the other hand, the view in 'Occupations Accessible to Women' is expressed in more formal language. Teaching is called 'both healthful and congenial', suggesting that it is a rewarding and pleasant profession.

40. Comparing perspective

1 For example: The writer of 'The Rearing and Management of Children' believes children need firm rules, whereas Simon Carr's perspective on parenting appears to be far less rigid.
2 For example: In 'The Rearing and Management of Children', the writer uses the emotive phrase 'a serious delusion', which helps to show the writer's strong feelings about obedience. In *The Boys Are Back in Town*, Carr uses more informal and colloquial phrases, such as 'pretty loose ship' and 'fuzzy logic', to show that he is more relaxed about the behaviour of his children.
3 Answers should consist of one P-E-E paragraph. The paragraph should use one piece of evidence from each of the extracts and suitable adverbials. Answers could include these key points:
- both texts maintain same perspective throughout
- Carr ends with a colloquial term 'semi-feral'
- 'The Rearing and Management of Children' ends with the formal phrase 'implanting a spirit of obedience'.

41. Answering a compare question

1 Answers should:
- compare the language in the two texts
- focus on the effect of the writer's language choices
- support key points with evidence and explanation/analysis.

42. Putting it into practice

1 Answers could include these key points:
The Boys are Back in Town:
- the writer has a relaxed attitude to parenting and believes children should not be too restricted by rules
- colloquial language – 'pretty loose ship', 'fuzzy logic'
- words that suggest sport – 'outer marker', 'boundaries', 'perimeter'
- one sentence paragraph – 'Fewer rules...'
- repetition of 'mothers' and 'routine'
- paragraph of lists using short sentences – 'No interrupting adults'
- words/phrases with animal connotations – 'Free-range', 'feral'.

'The Rearing and Management of Children':
- the writer feels that children should be given clear rules and boundaries
- repetition – 'No harsh words, no impatient gestures'
- formal language – 'habits of obedience'
- words/phrases with connotations of strictness and discipline – 'enforce the rules', 'requires great firmness in checking'
- detailed examples to back up points – 'Taking food as an example...'
- emotive language – 'depraved', 'exposed', 'rejected'.

43. Evaluating a text: fiction

1 All options should be circled except: 'Focus closely on individual words and phrases, explaining connotations in detail.' This should not be circled as it is only necessary to write about the **overall impression** created by a word/phrase, rather than writing in depth about language techniques and the connotations of individual words.

2 (a) 'We were all talking at once' – Answer provided on page 43 of Workbook
'myself and the motorist' links to 'he then puts himself first when explaining an idea'
'Someone ... Someone' links to 'The writer uses repetition'

(b) For example: The narrator does not appear to be a natural leader at the start of this section as he **admits he is the same as the other men when he says 'we were all talking at once'.**
However, he then puts himself first when explaining an idea, for example **in the phrase 'myself and the motorist'. This gives the impression that he feels his input is the most important.**
The writer uses repetition to **reinforce this idea that the narrator is the natural leader in the scene. The repeated word 'Someone' suggests that no one else stands out, as the other men are not given names.**

3 The evidence selected should recognise that the narrator is **not** shown to be a natural leader throughout the extract. For example: 'I must have been a hundred yards away when the situation came under control.'

44. Evaluating a text: non-fiction

1 **A4.** What do you think and feel about the <u>view of female teachers</u> presented in 'Occupations Accessible to Women'? **(10 marks)**
You should comment on:
- what is said
- how it is said

<u>You must refer to the text</u> to support your comments.

2 Overview C (because it is the most specific)

3 For example: The ending of the article suggests that the writer feels **that if women could 'manage to qualify' themselves sufficiently, then teaching would be an 'eminently tempting', attractive career for them. This indicates that the writer's viewpoint remains the same throughout the whole extract.**

45. Using evidence to evaluate

1 For example: The writer feels that women are so poorly educated that only 'hard study' will overcome the 'inaccuracy' of their knowledge. The writer feels this situation is serious as he states **that 'even the most highly-educated of women' are not adequately qualified.** The writer emphasises this negative view of women's education by suggesting that they cannot work **'with rapidity'** or **'explain ... clearly'**. This all suggests **that the writer has a very negative view of the way women have been educated.**

2 The writer feels that life for a female teacher can be very pleasant **as they earn a good salary, free accommodation is provided and some positions come with allowances for utility bills. Some teaching positions in larger towns are even more attractive as they offer higher salaries.**

3 (b) Include it as part of your sentence. (All other statements are things you **should** do when using longer quotations.)

46. Putting it into practice

1 Answers could include these key points:
- Shukhov does not get up straight away
- he has found a way to keep warm and ignore others – 'head buried in a blanket and a coat'
- he understands what happens in the camp – 'knew from the sounds', and list of what is happening outside his room
- he understands how hard the work is – 'digging holes, knocking in fence posts'
- Despite the hard work to come, he knows how to cope – 'dig, dig'
- he understands who to bribe to make life easier – 'slip the senior work-assigner half a kilo of fatback'
- the extract ends on this note – he knows how to get out of the work, 'wangle a day off'
- whole extract – most of the extract suggests he knows how the camp works and has come to terms with it.

47. Putting it into practice

1 Answers could include these key points:
- people who do not agree with strict discipline are suffering from a 'serious delusion', which suggests a great belief in the writer's own views
- strict discipline is the most important part of parenting – 'Obedience is the first lesson to be taught'
- the writer makes discipline sound simple – 'simply in not doing as the babe demands'
- even very young children should have discipline – 'mere babe'
- children cannot be trusted to make good choices – 'they would be eating and drinking perpetually'
- 'great firmness' must be used and parents must be very determined.

SECTION B: WRITING

48. Writing questions: an overview

1 (a) Component 1
(b) Component 2
(c) Component 2
(d) Component 1
(e) Component 1
(f) Component 2

2 (a) Assessment objective 5
(b) Both
(c) Assessment objective 6
(d) Assessment objective 6
(e) Assessment objective 5
(f) Assessment objective 5

3 For example:
Assessment objective 5 (a) – Write fluently and engagingly using appropriate techniques to suit a variety of audiences, purposes and styles.
Assessment objective 5 (b) – Arrange ideas effectively using appropriate techniques to ensure the text is clear.
Assessment objective 6 – Use a wide selection of words in a range of sentence styles, and accurate spelling and punctuation throughout.

49. Writing questions: Component 1

1 (a) True
(b) False
(c) False
(d) True

2 (a) story
(b) For example: A recount is a structured account of a personal experience. It does not need to be a true, real-life event.

3 (c) narrative or recount
4 story (narrative)
5

Planning your answer	10 minutes
Writing your answer	30 minutes
Checking and proofreading your answer	5 minutes

50. Writing questions: Component 2

1 formal / ~~informal~~
intended to achieve a specific purpose / ~~amusing and light-hearted~~
~~entertaining and humorous~~ / serious, with humour only if appropriate to audience
for a specific audience / ~~suitable for all ages~~
~~open-ended~~ / carefully structured

2 (a) These words should be circled: 'Headteacher/ Principal'
(b) This word should be circled in Question B1: 'report'
This word should be circled in Question B2: 'article'
(c) These words should be circled in Question B1: 'suggesting ways this might be done'
These words should be circled in Question B2: 'You could write in favour of or against this proposal'

3

	Question B1	Question B2
Planning your answer	5 minutes	5 minutes
Writing your answer	20 minutes	20 minutes
Checking and proofreading your answer	5 minutes	5 minutes

51. Writing for a purpose: creative

1 For example:
see: a kaleidoscope of brilliant colours
hear: screeching crowds on the rollercoasters
smell: Answer provided on page 51 of Workbook
touch: the excited grip of my sister's warm hand
taste: Answer provided on page 51 of Workbook

2 For example: My face lit up with a wide smile and **my excitement mounted as I pushed through the crowds and stole my first glimpse of the brightly lit rides.**

3 For example:
Simile: colours as bright and dazzling as a firework display
Metaphor: rides towering over us
Personification: the darkness swallowed us as our ride on the ghost train began

4 Answers should:
- use the senses
- include examples of figurative language
- include examples of carefully chosen language
- use verbs that show rather than tell
- maintain one narrative voice throughout.

For example: My face lit up with a wide smile and my excitement mounted as I pushed through the crowds and stole my first glimpse of the brightly lit rides. A kaleidoscope of colours as bright and dazzling as a firework display met my eager eyes and, inhaling deeply, I could almost taste the syrupy sweet candy-floss on sale nearby. I squeezed my sister's hand and grinned.

52. Writing for a purpose: inform, explain, review

1 (a) Answer provided on page 52 of Workbook
For example:
(b) What is already on offer
(c) New services for teenagers
(d) Teenager-friendly opening times

2 Remember that you can make facts and statistics up, as long as they are believable. For example:
(a) More than 50% of teenagers have not considered using the local library for study
(b) Over three-quarters of teenagers said they might use the local library if facilities were improved
(c) Extending opening times to 7pm would attract students after school hours
(d) 95% of all teenagers said they would be more likely to use the library if there was a special study zone

3 Answers might include sub-headings and should include examples of facts and statistics. The tone of the writing should be formal. For example:
The local library currently works hard to offer a broad and flexible service. Nonetheless, more than half of local teenagers have not considered using the facilities for study purposes. This suggests that, while the library's efforts to attract the attention of other sections of society have been successful, it is currently failing to appeal to those aged 18 and under.

53. Writing for a purpose: argue and persuade

1 Examples of points **for** the suggestion could include: people spend hours on the internet; like other addictive drugs, people's use increases the more they use it, meaning they become more and more dependent; people denied access can suffer cravings.
Examples of points **against** the suggestion could include: the time people spend on the internet shows how useful it is; it does not cause physical harm; using the internet is no different to reading a book or meeting friends, except it is onscreen.

2 Answers will vary. Remember that you can make evidence up, as long as it is believable. For example:
For the suggestion: point – people spend hours on the internet; evidence – 75% of all teenagers admit to spending at least two hours online every day.
Against the suggestion: point – using the internet is no different to reading a book or meeting friends, except it is onscreen; evidence – research conducted by Professor Nett and his team show that people who interact online rather than face-to-face have an equally healthy social life.

3 For example:
For – Some people might feel **that we spend too much time on the internet.** However, **it is clear from the number of hours that people spend online on a daily basis that the internet is an invaluable resource in the modern age.**
Against – Some people might feel **that the internet is not a danger as it does not cause physical harm.** However, **recent studies clearly show a rise in back, neck and wrist injuries resulting from extended periods in front of the screen and over-use of the mouse.**

4 For example (rhetorical device – list, as underlined):
Some people might feel **that the internet is not a danger as it does not cause physical harm.** However, **recent studies clearly show a rise in the numbers of internet users suffering from <u>back pain, repetitive strain injury in the wrist and forearm, blurred vision and poor concentration</u>.**

54. Writing for an audience

1 For example: The audience is likely to be **adults of both genders, probably those aged over 25, although younger people may read the article as it concerns them.**

2 Sentence B – The tone and vocabulary in this sentence are formal, which is appropriate for a national newspaper article whose audience is mainly adults.
3 Answers should be appropriate for a teenage audience, and may include some informal language although non-Standard English, including slang and texting language, should be avoided. A variety of sentence structures and a wide vocabulary should also be used. For example:
To begin with, while green, leafy vegetables may not appeal to your taste buds, they are nonetheless packed with fibre, vitamins and minerals. Their health benefits are widely acknowledged: apart from great skin and bundles of energy, these greens are thought to help protect you from diseases like diabetes, and possibly even cancer.

55. Putting it into practice

1 (a) Any of the four titles could be selected.
(b) Planning time: 10 minutes
Writing time: 30 minutes
Checking time: 5 minutes
Form: Should be suitable for the title chosen in part (a) and must be a narrative or a recount
Narrative voice: Should be suitable for the title chosen in part (a)
2 Examples of language techniques should be suitable for the title chosen in part 1 (a). Techniques used might include: using the senses, figurative language, language choice, etc.

56. Putting it into practice

1

	B1	**B2**
Timing	Plan: 5 minutes Write: 20 minutes Check: 5 minutes	Plan: 5 minutes Write: 20 minutes Check: 5 minutes
Topic	Role models for younger students	Dogs in parks
Form	Report	Newspaper article
Audience	Headteacher/ Principal	Probably adults of both genders
Purpose	To inform	To argue/persuade
Key features	Facts and statistics, tone, temporal adverbials, factual language	Key points, evidence, counter-arguments, adverbials, rhetorical devices

57. Form: articles and reviews

1–3 Answers will vary but should be suitable for an adult audience.
4 (The television programme on which this guided question is based is *I'm A Celebrity... Get Me Out Of Here!*) Answers should include a further two or three sentences containing figurative devices or language techniques, such as use of the senses, similes, metaphors and personification.

58. Form: letters and reports

1 (a) True
(b) True
(c) False (you should use 'Yours faithfully' if you have used 'Dear Sir/Madam')
(d) True
2 For example:
Heading: Youth Parliaments
Opening sentence: Many councils across the UK and Europe have set up youth parliaments and have found them to be an effective way to access the views of young people.
3 Answers should suggest two recommendations, which could include:
- setting up a Facebook page
- visiting schools and colleges.

59. Form: information guides

1 For example:
(a) Find it, see it, love it!
(b) What's going on and where to find it
(c) What's on, Sherlock?
2 For example: 'Find it, see it, love it!' would be most effective for a teenage audience because the pattern of three and the repetition of 'it' make it straight to the point as well as eye-catching.
3 For example:
(a) Answer provided on page 59 of Workbook
(b) Getting from A to B
(c) Eat, drink, enjoy
4 For example:
Read on to find out:
- what's on and where it is
- how to get around
- where to find the best food
- what not to miss.

Note that answers to Questions 1, 3 and 4 should use language and a tone that is suitable for a teenage audience – punchy and possibly with some informal language, but still in Standard English.

60. Putting it into practice

1 Answers should be suitable for an adult audience and should include:
- a title
- an introduction
- details of the current situation and some appropriate recommendations
- facts/statistics to support the recommendations
- a conclusion.

61. Ideas and planning: creative

1 Any of the four titles could be selected.
2 Answers will vary depending on the title chosen in Question 1, but all plans should answer key questions about the characters (e.g. who is there, what they are like) and the action (e.g. what is happening, what has happened already).
3 Details added to the plan should develop the idea of the trip and include examples of creative writing techniques, such as figurative devices and use of the senses. For example: Describe the journey, personification of aeroplane – whisks us away.

62. Structure: creative

1 Answers will vary but all should:
- complete the narrative structure with a balanced amount of detail for each stage
- include ideas about creative writing techniques.

For example:
Exposition: Relaxing in front of fire on windy winter day. Doorbell rings. I answer – it is my long-lost sister. Use dialogue to introduce her character.
Rising action: In kitchen, making tea – use senses. Sister starts to tell me where she's been all these years. Depict sister – show not tell, simile/metaphor to describe her manner.

Climax: Reveals she's been living in Peru, where she set up an organisation to help the poor; personification to express my surprise.
Falling action: She explains her project and its aims; use vivid vocabulary to picture the setting.
Resolution: She invites me to go out there for the summer to help with her work; action verbs.

2 As for Question 1. Answers should adapt the answer to Question 1 and follow the flashback structure given in the Workbook. For example:
Climax: Reveals she's been living in Peru, where she set up an organisation to help the poor; personification to express my surprise.
Exposition: Relaxing in front of fire on windy winter day. Doorbell rings. I answer – it is my long-lost sister. Use dialogue to introduce her character.
Rising action: In kitchen, making tea – use senses. Sister starts to tell me where she's been all these years. Depict sister – show not tell, simile/metaphor to describe her manner.
Return to climax: Sister telling me about Peru.
Falling action: She explains her project and its aims; use vivid vocabulary to picture the setting.
Resolution: She invites me to go out there for the summer to help with her work; action verbs.

63. Beginnings and endings: creative

1 Beginnings should not over-use dialogue and should contain appropriate figurative devices and language techniques. For example, for 'Conflict or danger':
The envelope burned in my hand. To open it was, I knew, to enter a different world where I would never be completely safe again. My heart thundered in my chest and my blood boiled past my ears.

2 Answers will vary depending on the opening chosen from Question 1.

3 Answers should reflect the tone decided on in Question 2.

64. Putting it into practice

1 Plans should include:
- some form of five-part narrative structure, for example, a spider diagram
- ideas for the beginning/ending
- details of narrative voice and creative writing techniques to be used.

65. Ideas and planning: inform, explain, review

1 Plans should include:
- an introduction and a conclusion
- three or four sequenced key points
- a range of supporting ideas and details.

66. Ideas and planning: argue and persuade

1 Plans should include:
- an introduction and a conclusion
- three sequenced key points
- supporting evidence
- a counter-argument.

67. Openings: transactional/persuasive

1 For example:
Rhetorical question – Is prison the answer to serious crime?
Bold or controversial statement – Prison has never been less effective in preventing serious crime.
Relevant quotation – 'Prison saved me. It turned my life around.'
Shocking or surprising fact or statistic – No less than 58% of offenders sentenced to less than a year in prison go on to reoffend.
Short, relevant, interesting anecdote – Answer provided on page 67 of Workbook

2 Answers will vary but all should:
- make clear the topic/argument
- include one or two of the suggested approaches from Question 1.

68. Conclusions: transactional/persuasive

1 For example:
Vivid image – As the colossal prison door swings shut behind yet another serial offender, so too does the window of opportunity to make a real change.
Warning – If alternatives to prison sentences are not found soon, serious crime rates will only continue to rise.
Happy note – Crime may not pay, but with serious crime rates on the decrease, sending offenders to prison certainly does.
Thought-provoking question – Answer provided on page 68 of Workbook
'Call to action' – We must call on the government to think again about their approach to prison sentences. Now is the time for change.
Refer to introduction – So, prison is not the whole answer to serious crime, but it is a vital part of the solution.

2 Answers will vary but all should include one or two of the suggested approaches from Question 1.

69. Putting it into practice

1 Plans should include:
- an engaging title
- sub-headings
- a rating
- an idea for an engaging opening paragraph
- ideas for about three sequenced paragraphs, with details of figurative language to be used
- an idea for the conclusion.

70. Paragraphing for effect

1 Point: 'When students choose their GCSE options' to 'help them in their future career'.
Evidence: 'I chose my GCSEs' to 'because lots of my friends had chosen that subject'.
Explanation: 'Neither of these reasons are sound' to 'more informed and more sensible decisions'.

2 For example:
Point: The careers advice currently available to students is inadequate.
Evidence: Students make poor choices about which subjects to continue to study.
Explanation: Students find themselves ill-prepared or unable to pursue the career that best suits them.

3 While schools and colleges do offer some careers advice to students, the advice is frequently inadequate, failing to outline clearly all possible career paths students may wish to follow. This is clear in the poor choices students make about which subjects to continue studying, which often do not support their ideal career. As a result, students find themselves ill-prepared or unable to pursue the career they are best suited to, a situation which could be prevented with more and improved careers advice.

4 Point: 'While schools and colleges' to 'may wish to follow'.
Evidence: 'This is clear' to 'their ideal career'.
Explanation: 'As a result' to 'improved careers advice'.

71. Linking ideas

1

Adding an idea	Explaining	Illustrating
Furthermore...	Consequently	For example
Moreover...	Therefore	For instance

Emphasising	Comparing	Contrasting
In particular	In the same way	However
Significantly	Similarly	On the other hand

2 Extract 1 examples: For example...; therefore...
Extract 2 examples: Moreover... ; Significantly...; ...for instance...
Extract 3 examples: However...

3 Answers will vary but all should use a P-E-E structure and feature a range of adverbials. For example:
Exams cannot give a fair and accurate picture of a student's real abilities as too much is dependent on the day of the exam and how the student is feeling on that particular day. For instance, a student might be highly competent and have worked hard to prepare for the exam. However, they may also have had a sleepless night or be struggling with an illness on the day of the exam, which may lead to poorer marks than they might otherwise have attained. Consequently, exams are not only an unrepresentative but also an unfair means of assessing a student's ability.

72. Putting it into practice

1 Answers should include:
- appropriate features for audience, purpose and format
- well-structured and sequenced paragraphs, with one main point or idea per paragraph
- a range of adverbials to link paragraphs and guide the reader.

73. Vocabulary for effect: synonyms

1 For example:
Students: pupils, exam candidates, learners
Improve: develop, enhance, extend
Learning: achievement, attainment, skills
Doing: completing, achieving, carrying out, performing

2 For example:

embarrassed	upset	scream	moment	annoyed
Answers provided on page 73 of Workbook	concerned worried alarmed	yell shriek shout	occasion time situation	aggravated agitated distressed

3 Answers will vary but all should include some of the synonyms from Question 2. For example:
On that day, on that occasion, I was mortified. I could have yelled or shouted, agitated as I was, but my sense of humiliation was total. I could barely manage a whisper. I tried to speak. Nothing. Alarmed at what they might be thinking, I took a deep breath and tried again.

74. Vocabulary for effect: argue and persuade

1 For example:
A – Answer provided on page 74 of Workbook
B – 'use too many' could be replaced by: devour, fritter away; 'not have enough food' could be replaced by: starve
C – 'filled with' could be replaced by: dominated by, ruled by; 'not like' could be replaced by: hate, detest; 'cannot do much about it' could be replaced by: are powerless to change it

2 (a) For example: The word 'roar' suggests a lion and has connotations of loudness, anger, aggression and dominance. This would suggest that some parents are determined to fight the plans and win.
(b) For example: The word 'howl' suggests loudness, though perhaps a loudness that is ineffective, which creates the impression that the parents are protesting but that the plans will go ahead.
(c) The word 'whimper' suggests weakness and that the parents do not present a real opposition to the school's plans.

3 Answers will vary but all should consist of two sentences and include vocabulary chosen for its impact and connotations. For example:
There are those who feel that social networking is a colossal waste of time, squandering the precious hours we might otherwise lavish on worthier pursuits. Yet, for many, social networks are a lifeline, a vital connection with those on whose friendship and support they rely.

75. Language for different effects 1

1 Extract A – rhetorical question
Extract B – contrast, list, repetition
Extract C – contrast, list
Extract D – contrast
Extract E – contrast, list, repetition
Extract F – repetition

2 Answers will vary but all should consist of four short extracts. Each extract should use one or more of the language techniques explored in Question 1.
For example:
Contrast: Young new drivers are often over-confident, in spite of the fact that they are unpractised and uncertain in many of the traffic situations they find themselves in.
Repetition: We let 18-year-olds buy cigarettes. We let 18-year-olds buy alcohol. We let 18-year-olds vote. Young people should not have to wait until they are 21 to take their driving test.
Rhetorical question: Why has it taken so long for us to consider this crucial proposal?
List: At 17, teenagers are simply too immature, irresponsible, self-centred and impulsive to be allowed behind the wheel of a car.

76. Language for different effects 2

1 Extract A – hyperbole, alliteration
Extract B – direct address (and a rhetorical question)
Extract C – alliteration, pattern of three
Extract D – hyperbole
Extract E – pattern of three
Extract F – direct address

2 Answers will vary but all should consist of four short extracts. Each extract should use one or more of the language techniques explored in Question 1. For example:
Direct address: Do you really believe that our schools, the centres of learning that open for us so many doors of opportunity and of possibility, can be considered cruel?
Pattern of three: School is vital in teaching us to ask questions, seek answers and use our understanding to make the world a better place.
Alliteration: The cruelty of our crusty and crumbling school regime is designed to cripple the imagination and crush the soul.
Hyperbole: School is undoubtedly the cruellest and most confining form of imprisonment and torture found in the world today.

77. Language for different effects 3

1 Extract A – personification
Extract B – metaphor
Extract C – simile
Extract D – Answer provided on page 77 of Workbook
Extract E – metaphor
Extract F – personification

2 Answers will vary but all should consist of four short extracts. Each extract should use one of the figurative devices explored in Question 1.
For example:
Simile: It is as clear as a recently cleaned window that the best way to engage students in their learning is to get on with the day as early as possible.
Metaphor: The current early start to the school day is the weight around the ankles of all those of us who are not naturally early risers.
Personification: The longer students are given in the morning, the longer their duvets will pin them down and prevent them from getting up at all.
Simile and personification: Teenagers are as sleepy as dormice and, ring as it might, an alarm clock frequently lacks the strength to drag them out of their slumber by itself.

78. Using the senses

1 Any two of the extracts should be circled, according to personal preference.

2 Answers will vary according to the extracts chosen in Question 1, but explanations should reflect the 'show not tell' technique of using the senses.

3 Answers will vary but all should:
- consist of one paragraph
- use at least three of the senses and the 'show not tell' technique
- include examples of figurative language such as similes, metaphors and personification.

For example:
My skin prickled. Again the whining creak of the stair pierced the silence. I froze, half squatting, half kneeling on the icy slabs. As dark as pitch, the house waited and I, a frightened animal, held my breath.

79. Narrative voice

1 Extract A – first person
Extract B – answer provided on p. 79 of Workbook
Extract C – first person
Extract D – third person

2 Answers will vary but all should consist of two possible openings. Each opening should:
- consist of one or two sentences
- use a different narrative voice.

For example: I opened the door to discarded food, bottles, cans, clothes and even parts of a bicycle, all strewn haphazardly over the filthy carpet. As I crunched what looked distinctly like part of my mother's best dinner service under my foot, I realised the time had come to make a stand.

80. Putting it into practice

1 Answers should include examples of:
- language appropriate to format, audience and purpose
- language chosen for effect
- figurative devices
- language techniques, e.g. rhetorical questions, patterns of three, etc.

81. Putting it into practice

1 Answers should include:
- language appropriate to the audience
- ambitious and effective language choices
- a range of language techniques, including figurative devices
- a consistent narrative voice.

82. Sentence variety 1

1 (a) B (multi-clause sentence with subordinate clause); it has two clauses, one of which is subordinate, linked with *because*
(b) E (minor sentence); it has no verb
(c) C (multi-clause sentence with coordinate clause); it has an equal pair of clauses, linked with *but*
(d) Answer provided on page 82
(e) D (multi-clause sentence with relative clause); the clause introduced by the relative pronoun *which*, is separated from the main clause with commas

2 For example: Professional footballers are possibly the worst 'fakers'. With just one tap from another player they fall over, dive to the ground or occasionally fly. They always start screaming because it shows they are seriously injured. They say it was a foul. They demand a free kick. Ridiculous.

83. Sentence variety 2

1 For example:
(a) A pronoun – Answer provided on page 83 of Workbook
(b) An article – The big city with its bright lights and busy sounds is without a doubt the place for me.
(c) A preposition – Between the closely stacked tower blocks, you can just make out the occasional grey of the Thames.
(d) An -ing word (or present participle) – Crawling around the congested ring road in the sultry summer heat, I dream of country air and open spaces.
(e) An adjective – Slow is not a word for the big city, where speed is everything.
(f) An adverb – Happily, my flat is down a quiet side road and so the sounds of the city are subdued.
(g) A conjunction – Although I spent my childhood on a farm, city life suits me surprisingly well.

2 Answers will vary but all should aim to:
- include all seven different types of sentence opener from Question 1
- use a different word to start each sentence.

For example: **I** grew up in a tiny village in the middle of nowhere. **Although**, after such quiet beginnings, I was attracted by the hustle and bustle of city life, I know now that my heart belongs in the country. **The** city, with its bright lights and busy sounds, is suffocating to me. **Between** the closely stacked tower blocks, I peer in vain for a glimpse of the river and the hills, and only occasionally am I rewarded. **Walking** home after work last night, I raised my head to the stars of the winter sky and imagined myself at home, where the only hurry is in the current of the stream that runs through our meadow. **Slow** is not a word for the big city. **Unexpectedly**, however, as I raised my head, something wonderful happened.

84. Sentences for different effects

1 The effect of the long sentence is that it emphasises the chain of events, and builds tension as the situation worsens.

The effect of the short sentence is that it brings the scene to an abrupt end, focusing on the narrator's horror.

2 Sentence A – emphasises 'her' unsympathetic reaction
Sentence B – emphasises the long walk home
Note that the information the writer wants to emphasise usually comes at the end of the sentence.

3 Answers will vary but all should aim to include a:
- long sentence followed by a short sentence
- sentence structured to give specific emphasis.

For example: Just for a moment, imagine that you have to face each day with a disability or a life-limiting condition, that each day presents a risk of exploitation or violence, or that you feel isolated, alone and are vulnerable. Imagine you are a child in need. Children in Need is a wonderful charity through which you and I, our friends and families, our neighbours and neighbourhoods, in fact, every one of us can make a difference.

85. Putting it into practice

1 Answers should include examples of:
- a range of sentence types
- sentences beginning in a range of different ways
- sentences structured for effect.

86. Ending a sentence

1 At the end of a sentence
2 At the end of a question
3 (a) Answer provided on page 86 of Workbook
(b) Avoid using them for anything other than an exclamation
(c) Avoid using two or more exclamation marks in a row
4 Sentence A is incorrect. This is a comma splice: two sentences are joined with a comma and they should be separated with a full stop or joined with a conjunction.
Sentence B is correct. The two sentences are separated with a full stop.
Sentence C is correct. The two sentences are joined with a conjunction.
5 There are eight mistakes in total in the original, including the unnecessary exclamation marks at the end of the title:

<u>A Change of Heart</u> **[1]**
I braced myself for a confrontation. **[2]** *She was looking at me like she knew I had something to say and she didn't want to hear it. My heart began to race and a strange throbbing pain pulsed in my forehead. How could I say it?* **[3]** *How could I tell her what I was thinking without upsetting her?* **[4]** *She knew something was coming.* **[5]** *Tears were welling up in her dark brown eyes and her bottom lip was starting to quiver. I didn't feel much better than she did.* **[6]** *My stomach was churning and I could feel my legs shaking. I tried to speak.* **[7]** *My mouth felt like sandpaper.* **[8]** *It was dry and rough and I couldn't form the words.*

87. Commas

1–2 A Incorrect: They can comfort us in a crisis**, [comma needed here]** help out when we're in trouble**, [comma needed here]** or make us laugh or make us cry.
B Correct
C Correct
D Answer given on p. 87 of Workbook
E Correct
F Incorrect: Although I had known her since primary school**, [comma needed here]** we never spoke again.
G Incorrect: The problem**, [comma needed here]** which we may not want to face, is that friends can sometimes let us down.
H Incorrect: A friend**, [comma needed here]** who I will not name**, [comma needed here]** once told me all my worst faults.
I Correct

3 Answers will vary but all should aim to use commas correctly to separate:
- items in a list
- a main and subordinate clause
- a main and relative clause.

For example: When I think back, I know that Alice was the perfect friend. Funny, clever, unswervingly loyal and eminently talented, Alice was also one of the kindest people I have ever known. One day, I admired, with considerable feelings of envy, her violin. Without a moment of hesitation, Alice passed me the instrument, which was a valuable family heirloom, and encouraged me to try it out.

88. Apostrophes and speech punctuation

1–2 A – Incorrect: should be *don't*
B – Correct
C – Incorrect: should be *wouldn't*
D – Incorrect: should be *teacher's* because it is singular (one teacher)
E – Correct
F – Correct (plural: several boys' faces)
G – Correct
H – Correct
I – Incorrect: 'Come over here**, [comma needed here]**' *he whispered.*

3 Answers will vary but all should aim to use apostrophes and speech marks correctly. For example:
'Hey,' she called. 'Come over here.'
'What do you want?' I asked**, full of curiosity.**
'Have you heard about Adam?'
'No, nothing. What about him?'
'Keep your voice down!' she hissed, 'People will hear.'
'Hear what exactly?' I whispered, beginning to feel a little impatient.
'Well, you know what he's been like lately. Apparently, more than one teacher has phoned his parents to complain.'
'I'm not surprised,' I said, wondering what all the fuss was about.

89. Colons, semi-colons, dashes, brackets and ellipses

1 For example:
A – There is only one thing you can do to improve your grades**: [colon, followed by lower case r for revise]** revise.
B – Teachers can help**: [colon, followed by lower case t for they]** they can give revision tips and answer any questions you have about the exam.
C – Revision isn't easy**: [colon, followed by lower case i for it]** it takes time and willpower.
D – Exams are the problem**; [semi-colon, followed by lower case r for revision]** revision is the solution.

2–3 A – Correct
B – Correct
C – Incorrect: *My bedroom walls are covered in scribbled revision notes and key points – not a pretty sight*. (Brackets **must** be used in pairs; dashes can be used singly.)
D – Answer given on p. 89 of Workbook

4 Answers will vary but all should aim to use:
- a colon and a semi-colon
- dashes, brackets and an ellipsis.

For example: Deep breathing, positive mantras and assertive body language: this was Day One of the new me. I had never been a very confident person;

I often struggled to believe in myself and in my own abilities. Yet, for a long time, it had been clear to me that something needed to change – and to change for the better. Many of my friends encouraged me, urging me on with warm words of support, while others (including my own mother) doubted I had the will power to turn the corner. As I started to put the plans in place, I wondered who would turn out to be right…

90. Putting it into practice

1 Answers should feature a range of punctuation used accurately, including advanced punctuation, such as colons and semi-colons.

91. Common spelling errors 1

1 Sentence A – *their* (not there)
Sentence B – *would have* (not *would of*); *absolutely* (not *absolutley*)
Sentence C – *effect* (not *affect*); *extremely* (not *extremley*)
Sentence D – Correct
Sentence E – *There are* (not *Their our*)
Sentence F – *They're* (not *There*)
Sentence G – *its* (not *it's*)
Sentence H – *definitely* have (not *definitley* of)
Sentence I – *It's* (not *Its*); *are affected* (not *our effected*)
Sentence J – *our* (not *are*)
Sentence K – *could not have been* (not *could not of been*); *their* (not *there*)
Sentence L – *negatively* (not *negativley*)
Sentence M – *It's* (not *Its*)

92. Common spelling errors 2

1 Sentence A – *where* (not *were*); *whose* (not *who's*)
Sentence B – *Too* (not *To*)
Sentence C – *passed* (not *past*)
Sentence D – *pressure off us* (not *pressure of us*)
Sentence E – *You're* (not *Your*)
Sentence F – *Who's* (not *Whose*)
Sentence G – *were* (not *where*)
Sentence H – *past* (not *passed*); *were* (not wear)
Sentence I – *to an extreme* (not *too an extreme*)
Sentence J – Correct
Sentence K – *you're* (not *your*)
Sentence L – *off* (not *of*)
Sentence M – *we're* (not *were*)

93. Common spelling errors 3

1 argument
difficult
disappoint
disappear
embarrassing
possession
beginning
recommend
occasionally
definitely
separately
conscious
conscience
experience
independence
believe
weird
business
rhythm
decision
grateful

2 Spelling practised will vary depending on the errors found in Question 1.

94. Proofreading

1 The corrections are shown in **bold**.
Scotland is the most amazing place **I've** ever visite**d.** **Even** though it took ten hours to drive **there,** it was worth it the moment **I** saw **where** we were staying**:** huge blue lochs, rolling green hills, miles and miles of pine forest. They even looked beautiful driving **past** them in a car.
On the first **day,** we took the dogs for a long walk through a forest**.** **It** was the **quietest** place **I've** ever been. Even with my brother **there**, all you could hear was the sound of **leaves** rustling in the breeze, the birds singing and **your** heart beating.
Our hotel was great**;** the **Scottish** people are so **friendly**. I would **definitely** stay there again.

2 Answers will vary depending on the work chosen.

3 Spelling practised will vary depending on the errors found in Question 2.

95. Putting it into practice

1 Answers should feature accurately used spelling, punctuation and grammar, and possibly signs of going back through the answer in order to make corrections.

For your own notes

For your own notes

For your own notes

For your own notes

For your own notes

For your own notes

Published by Pearson Education Limited, 80 Strand, London, WC2R 0RL.

www.pearsonschoolsandfecolleges.co.uk

Typeset by Tech-Set Ltd, Gateshead

Produced by Out of House Publishing

Illustrated by Tech-Set Ltd, Gateshead

Cover illustration by Miriam Sturdee

First published 2015

24

10 9 8 7 6 5

British Library Cataloguing in Publication Data

A catalogue record for this book is available from the British Library

ISBN 9781447987956

Printed in Great Britain by Bell and Bain Ltd, Glasgow

Acknowledgements

We are grateful to the following for permission to reproduce copyright material:

Extract on page 96 from *A Day in the Life of Ivan Denisovich*, Orion Publishing Group (Solzhenitsyn A); Extract on page 101 from 'appy Ever After, *The Sunday Times*, 30/11/2014 (Arlidge J) News UK; Extract on page 97 from *To Kill a Mockingbird*, Arrow Books (Lee H) Penguin Random House and HarperCollins US; Extract on page 103 from OK, you try teaching 13-year-olds, *The Guardian* (Hanson M) The Guardian; Extract on page 98 from *The Day of the Triffids*, Viking Books (Wyndham J) David Higham; Extract on page 100 Excerpt(s) from THE BOYS ARE BACK by Simon Carr, copyright © 2000 by Simon Carr. Used by permission of Vintage Books, an imprint of the Knopf Doubleday Publishing Group, division of Penguin Random House LLC. All rights reserved; Extract on page 99 Excerpt(s) from ENDURING LOVE by Ian McEwan, copyright © 1997 by Ian McEwan. Used by permission of Doubleday, an imprint of the Knopf Doubleday Publishing Group, a division of Penguin Random House LLC. All rights reserved. Extract on page 106-108 from *I'm the King of the Castle*, Longman (Hill S) Sheil Land Associates Ltd; Extract on page 112 from The extraordinary story behind Danny Boyle's 127 Hours, *The Guardian,* 15/12/2010 (Barkham P) The Guardian.